Sword Drills
Bible Exercises for the Spiritual Warrior

Rev. Michael Dorsey

A companion journal to How To Study Your Bible,

volume 1 of the How To Live series

This book is a companion to volume 1 of the How To Live series:

volume 1	How To Study Your Bible
volume 2	How To Pray
volume 3	How To Be Blessed
volume 4	How To Please God
volume 5	How To Flow
volume 6	How To Get Healed
volume 7	How To Be Right
volume 8	How To Love
volume 9	How To Worship
Volume 10	How To Rule

Sword Drills: Exercises for the Spiritual Warrior
ISBN 978-0-9916205-5-5

Copyright © 2016 by Robert Michael Dorsey

Published by Malakim Press
PO Box 456
Aberdeen, MD 21001

Cover art and design by Rose Watters

Cover photo and back cover photo by Jamal Lawson - http://www.jamallawson.com

Table of Contents

Introduction

Welcome to *Sword Drills: Exercises for the Spiritual Warrior.* This workbook is designed to accompany my book *How To Study Your Bible,* but it can also be used as a stand-alone book of activities to improve your Bible study skills. However, in order to make it a viable stand-alone workbook, a small portion of *How To Study Your Bible* has been duplicated in *Sword Drills.*

When I was a little boy in Sunday School, we would sometimes compete in a game called Sword Drills, where the teacher would have two children stand up in the front of the room with our Bibles. We would be given a Scripture reference and then we had to race to try to be the first to find it. If you lost then you had to sit down, but if you won, then the other kid would sit down and another one would come forward to become your new opponent for the next round. This game taught us how to find our way around the Bible quickly, and became the inspiration for the title of this work.

This book began as a 4-week course I taught at Riverside Church in the summer of 2013. In the original course, we covered information about the Bible, Bible study tools, and Bible study methods. That material is all included in the book *How To Study Your Bible.*

The students also did hands-on exercises during the class to learn the various different Bible study methods. These were targeted exercises designed to practice those new Bible study methods that we had just discussed for that lesson. Those exercises have been expanded to create *Sword Drills.*

It's one thing to talk about Bible study methods and to understand them conceptually, but it's another thing to actually perform exercises based on those methods by putting your own hand to paper. By the time you've finished reading this book, not only will you no longer be intimidated by the Bible, but you'll be fully equipped with a new spiritual tool belt that will enable you to mine the Word of God for nuggets of revelation that you can then easily apply to your own life.

There's no reason you can't become a skilled Bible student in your own right. Just take the exercises revealed in this workbook and apply them to the parts of the Bible that interest you the most. You can also use these exercises to gain a better understanding of more difficult passages that have challenged you in the past.

With greater understanding, you will find a greater comfort with the Bible. With greater comfort will come greater enthusiasm, and with greater enthusiasm will come greater proficiency at Bible study. Once you become proficient at Bible study, God will bless your determination with fresh revelation from the treasure of His Word.

So draw your sword (get your Bible out), and get ready to begin your *Sword Drills!*

Michael Dorsey

August 2016

Chapter 1

Devotional Bible Reading

Like newborn babies [you should] long for the pure milk of the word, so that by it you may be nurtured and grow in respect to salvation [its ultimate fulfillment] - 1 Peter 2:2 (AMP)

Devotional Bible reading simply means devoting yourself to reading a portion of the Scriptures each day. One reason why you need to find a Bible that you really enjoy using is because you'll be reading it every day during your devotional time.

Devotional reading isn't technically a method of Bible study per se. You will come across things during your devotional reading that interest you, topics which you may decide to study out later, but the purpose of your devotional reading time isn't to study.

You'll Need A Good Plan

The purpose of devotional Bible reading is simply to expose yourself to God's Word on a daily basis. You can't help but be changed on the inside when you're exposed to the light of the living Word, and the more you're exposed, the more you'll change and grow for the better. To help you expose yourself to the Scriptures every day, I want to share with you the daily Bible reading plan I follow.

Reading the Bible every day will enhance your spiritual growth more than anything else you'll do this year. However, even with a plan to follow, many believers are challenged to get through the entire Bible in one year. They start off strong with the best of intentions, but they get bogged down in Leviticus or Deuteronomy and then they get discouraged and quit.

Why This Bible Reading Plan Is Different

My Bible Reading Plan is different from most. It doesn't follow the Bible order straight through, but instead I've intentionally mixed things up. This way the more difficult portions of the Bible aren't all lumped together, and it also adds variety to your daily Bible reading. You don't sit down to dinner and eat all of your meat first, then finish your entire drink before moving on to eat your vegetables all at once, so why should your spiritual meals be that way? Instead, here's what you will do:

Each day you'll read up to five chapters: one chapter from Proverbs, one chapter of poetry (from Psalms or Ecclesiastes), two chapters from the remainder of the Old Testament, and one chapter from the New Testament. If you're a new believer and five chapters per day sounds too ambitious for you, then you can start smaller and work your way up to that. The main thing is that you're taking the Word of God into your Spirit and you're doing it consistently every day.

Proverbs

The Book of Proverbs consists of a series of stand-alone one liner verses that are designed to give you wisdom that will be relevant to your everyday life. If you're a new believer just starting out, I recommend you read at least one chapter from Proverbs and the New Testament columns each day. To me, Proverbs are the vitamins of your spiritual diet, both nourishing your spirit and building up your resistance to the counterfeit wisdom of this world. Proverbs has 31 chapters, so just read one chapter each day of the month: Chapter 1 on the 1st, chapter 2 on the

2nd, etc. and by the year's end you'll have read through Proverbs about 12 times!

Old Testament

All of the authors of the New Testament assume their readers are already familiar with the Old Testament. That's why it's very important that you are exposed to these writings so that you'll be able to fully understand all of the New Testament references to the Old. Each day you'll read 2-3 chapters from the Old Testament, so that you will have covered all of the Pentateuch, the historical books, and the prophets by the end of the year.

Poetry

Your daily chapter from the poetry column comes from either Psalms or Ecclesiastes, with the very long chapter of Psalm 119 divided up over several days. These books help you connect with God on an emotional level, and will be refreshing to read after you finish your two Old Testament chapters. At the end of the year you will have enjoyed both of these books twice with this plan.

New Testament

Finally, each day you'll read one chapter from the New Testament. Since there are more days in the year than chapters in the New Testament, I double up on the four Gospels (covering the life and ministry of Jesus Christ) and the Book of Romans. Romans is the pinnacle of the Apostle Paul's writings, and if you had no Bible, but only his letter to the Romans, it contains enough revelation for you to be saved. In addition to the Gospels and Romans, you will also have read Acts and the rest of the New Testament by the time you finish the year.

Hear the Word Daily

When you do your daily Bible reading, read the words out loud. The Word of God says that "... the ear tests words as the palate tastes food." (Job 34:3). If you're at work or a public place, at least whisper the words under your breath so you can hear them. This is important because hearing the Word is what will feed your spirit. Read silently if you have to, but if you can read out loud so you can hear it with your own ears, that's better. "So faith comes by hearing, and hearing by the word of Christ." (Romans 10:17)

People often ask me what my secret is to understanding the things of God. They have a hunger to experience spiritual growth, but I can tell when they ask me this question that they're looking for some magic bullet, and when I tell them the two things that will make more of a difference in their spiritual walk than anything else (consistent daily Bible reading and prayer), they often seem disappointed, as if they were looking for something deeper and more profound. Yet the truth of the matter is this: NOTHING will impact your own personal spiritual growth over time as much as daily Bible reading and prayer. I pray you enjoy your devotional Bible reading throughout this year!

Exercise 1-1

Tools needed: *Your Bible, this Bible Reading plan*

Start making time for devotional Bible reading on a daily basis. Start with whatever day it is now. Don't worry about starting from the beginning, just get started and read consistently every day!

January

Date	Wisdom	Old Testament	Poetry	New Testament
January 1	Proverbs 1	Genesis 1-2	Psalm 1	Matthew 1
January 2	Proverbs 2	Genesis 3-4	Psalm 2	Matthew 2
January 3	Proverbs 3	Genesis 5-6	Psalm 3	Matthew 3
January 4	Proverbs 4	Genesis 7-8	Psalm 4	Matthew 4
January 5	Proverbs 5	Genesis 9-10	Psalm 5	Matthew 5
January 6	Proverbs 6	Genesis 11-12	Psalm 6	Matthew 6
January 7	Proverbs 7	Genesis 13-14	Psalm 7	Matthew 7
January 8	Proverbs 8	Genesis 15-16	Psalm 8	Matthew 8
January 9	Proverbs 9	Genesis 17-18	Psalm 9	Matthew 9
January 10	Proverbs 10	Genesis 19-20	Psalm 10	Matthew 10
January 11	Proverbs 11	Genesis 21-22	Psalm 11	Matthew 11
January 12	Proverbs 12	Genesis 23-24	Psalm 12	Matthew 12
January 13	Proverbs 13	Genesis 25-26	Psalm 13	Matthew 13
January 14	Proverbs 14	Genesis 27-28	Psalm 14	Matthew 14
January 15	Proverbs 15	Genesis 29-30	Psalm 15	Matthew 15
January 16	Proverbs 16	Genesis 31-32	Psalm 16	Matthew 16
January 17	Proverbs 17	Genesis 33-34	Psalm 17	Matthew 17
January 18	Proverbs 18	Genesis 35-36	Psalm 18	Matthew 18
January 19	Proverbs 19	Genesis 37-38	Psalm 19	Matthew 19
January 20	Proverbs 20	Genesis 39-40	Psalm 20	Matthew 20
January 21	Proverbs 21	Genesis 41-42	Psalm 21	Matthew 21
January 22	Proverbs 22	Genesis 43-44	Psalm 22	Matthew 22
January 23	Proverbs 23	Genesis 45-46	Psalm 23	Matthew 23
January 24	Proverbs 24	Genesis 47-48	Psalm 24	Matthew 24
January 25	Proverbs 25	Genesis 49-50	Psalm 25	Matthew 25
January 26	Proverbs 26	Exodus 1-2	Psalm 26	Matthew 26
January 27	Proverbs 27	Exodus 3-4	Psalm 27	Matthew 27
January 28	Proverbs 28	Exodus 5-6	Psalm 28	Matthew 28
January 29	Proverbs 29	Exodus 7-8	Psalm 29	Mark 1
January 30	Proverbs 30	Exodus 9-10	Psalm 30	Mark 2
January 31	Proverbs 31	Exodus 11-12	Psalm 31	Mark 3

February

Date	Wisdom	Old Testament	Poetry	New Testament
February 1	Proverbs 1	Exodus 13-14	Psalm 32	Mark 4
February 2	Proverbs 2	Exodus 15-16	Psalm 33	Mark 5
February 3	Proverbs 3	Exodus 17-18	Psalm 34	Mark 6
February 4	Proverbs 4	Exodus 19-20	Psalm 35	Mark 7
February 5	Proverbs 5	Exodus 21-22	Psalm 36	Mark 8
February 6	Proverbs 6	Exodus 23-24	Psalm 37	Mark 9
February 7	Proverbs 7	Exodus 25-26	Psalm 38	Mark 10
February 8	Proverbs 8	Exodus 27-28	Psalm 39	Mark 11
February 9	Proverbs 9	Exodus 29-30	Psalm 40	Mark 12
February 10	Proverbs 10	Exodus 31-32	Psalm 41	Mark 13
February 11	Proverbs 11	Exodus 33-34	Psalm 42	Mark 14
February 12	Proverbs 12	Exodus 35-36	Psalm 43	Mark 15
February 13	Proverbs 13	Exodus 37-38	Psalm 44	Mark 16
February 14	Proverbs 14	Exodus 39-40	Psalm 45	Luke 1
February 15	Proverbs 15	Leviticus 1-2	Psalm 46	Luke 2
February 16	Proverbs 16	Leviticus 3-4	Psalm 47	Luke 3
February 17	Proverbs 17	Leviticus 5-6	Psalm 48	Luke 4
February 18	Proverbs 18	Leviticus 7-8	Psalm 49	Luke 5
February 19	Proverbs 19	Leviticus 9-10	Psalm 50	Luke 6
February 20	Proverbs 20	Leviticus 11-12	Psalm 51	Luke 7
February 21	Proverbs 21	Leviticus 13-14	Psalm 52	Luke 8
February 22	Proverbs 22	Leviticus 15-16	Psalm 53	Luke 9
February 23	Proverbs 23	Leviticus 17-18	Psalm 54	Luke 10
February 24	Proverbs 24	Leviticus 19-20	Psalm 55	Luke 11
February 25	Proverbs 25	Leviticus 21-22	Psalm 56	Luke 12
February 26	Proverbs 26	Leviticus 23-24	Psalm 57	Luke 13
February 27	Proverbs 27	Leviticus 25-26	Psalm 58	Luke 14
February 28	Proverbs 28	Lev. 27, Num. 1	Psalm 59	Luke 15

March

Date	Wisdom	Old Testament	Poetry	New Testament
March 1	Proverbs 1	Numbers 2-3	Psalm 60	Luke 16
March 2	Proverbs 2	Numbers 4-5	Psalm 61	Luke 17
March 3	Proverbs 3	Numbers 6-7	Psalm 62	Luke 18
March 4	Proverbs 4	Numbers 8-9	Psalm 63	Luke 19
March 5	Proverbs 5	Numbers 10-11	Psalm 64	Luke 20
March 6	Proverbs 6	Numbers 12-13	Psalm 65	Luke 21
March 7	Proverbs 7	Numbers 14-15	Psalm 66	Luke 22
March 8	Proverbs 8	Numbers 16-17	Psalm 67	Luke 23
March 9	Proverbs 9	Numbers 18-19	Psalm 68	Luke 24
March 10	Proverbs 10	Numbers 20-21	Psalm 69	John 1
March 11	Proverbs 11	Numbers 22-23	Psalm 70	John 2
March 12	Proverbs 12	Numbers 24-25	Psalm 71	John 3
March 13	Proverbs 13	Numbers 26-27	Psalm 72	John 4
March 14	Proverbs 14	Numbers 28-29	Psalm 73	John 5
March 15	Proverbs 15	Numbers 30-31	Psalm 74	John 6
March 16	Proverbs 16	Numbers 32-33	Psalm 75	John 7
March 17	Proverbs 17	Numbers 34-35	Psalm 76	John 8
March 18	Proverbs 18	Num. 36, Deut. 1	Psalm 77	John 9
March 19	Proverbs 19	Deut. 2-3	Psalm 78	John 10
March 20	Proverbs 20	Deut. 4-5	Psalm 79	John 11
March 21	Proverbs 21	Deut. 6-7	Psalm 80	John 12
March 22	Proverbs 22	Deut. 8-9	Psalm 81	John 13
March 23	Proverbs 23	Deut. 10-11	Psalm 82	John 14
March 24	Proverbs 24	Deut. 12-13	Psalm 83	John 15
March 25	Proverbs 25	Deut. 14-15	Psalm 84	John 16
March 26	Proverbs 26	Deut. 16-17	Psalm 85	John 17
March 27	Proverbs 27	Deut. 18-19	Psalm 86	John 18
March 28	Proverbs 28	Deut. 20-21	Psalm 87	John 19
March 29	Proverbs 29	Deut. 22-23	Psalm 88	John 20
March 30	Proverbs 30	Deut. 24-25	Psalm 89	John 21
March 31	Proverbs 31	Deut. 26-27	Psalm 90	Acts 1

April

Date	Wisdom	Old Testament	Poetry	New Testament
April 1	Proverbs 1	Deut. 28-29	Psalm 91	Acts 2
April 2	Proverbs 2	Deut. 30-31	Psalm 92	Acts 3
April 3	Proverbs 3	Deut. 32-33	Psalm 93	Acts 4
April 4	Proverbs 4	Deut. 34, Josh. 1	Psalm 94	Acts 5
April 5	Proverbs 5	Joshua 2-3	Psalm 95	Acts 6
April 6	Proverbs 6	Joshua 4-5	Psalm 96	Acts 7
April 7	Proverbs 7	Joshua 6-7	Psalm 97	Acts 8
April 8	Proverbs 8	Joshua 8-9	Psalm 98	Acts 9
April 9	Proverbs 9	Joshua 10-11	Psalm 99	Acts 10
April 10	Proverbs 10	Joshua 12-13	Psalm 100	Acts 11
April 11	Proverbs 11	Joshua 14-15	Psalm 101	Acts 12
April 12	Proverbs 12	Joshua 16-17	Psalm 102	Acts 13
April 13	Proverbs 13	Joshua 18-19	Psalm 103	Acts 14
April 14	Proverbs 14	Joshua 20-21	Psalm 104	Acts 15
April 15	Proverbs 15	Joshua 22-23	Psalm 105	Acts 16
April 16	Proverbs 16	Josh. 24, Judges 1	Psalm 106	Acts 17
April 17	Proverbs 17	Judges 2-3	Psalm 107	Acts 18
April 18	Proverbs 18	Judges 4-5	Psalm 108	Acts 19
April 19	Proverbs 19	Judges 6-7	Psalm 109	Acts 20
April 20	Proverbs 20	Judges 8-9	Psalm 110	Acts 21
April 21	Proverbs 21	Judges 10-11	Psalm 111	Acts 22
April 22	Proverbs 22	Judges 12-13	Psalm 112	Acts 23
April 23	Proverbs 23	Judges 14-15	Psalm 113	Acts 24
April 24	Proverbs 24	Judges 16-17	Psalm 114	Acts 25
April 25	Proverbs 25	Judges 18-19	Psalm 115	Acts 26
April 26	Proverbs 26	Judges 20-21	Psalm 116	Acts 27
April 27	Proverbs 27	Ruth 1-2	Psalm 117	Acts 28
April 28	Proverbs 28	Ruth 3-4	Psalm 118	Romans 1
April 29	Proverbs 29	I Samuel 1-2	Ps 119 (Aleph)	Romans 2
April 30	Proverbs 30	I Samuel 3-4	Ps 119 (Beth)	Romans 3

May

Date	Wisdom	Old Testament	Poetry	New Testament
May 1	Proverbs 1	I Samuel 5-6	Ps 119 (Gimel)	Romans 4
May 2	Proverbs 2	I Samuel 7-8	Ps 119 (Daleth)	Romans 5
May 3	Proverbs 3	I Samuel 9-10	Ps 119 (He)	Romans 6
May 4	Proverbs 4	I Samuel 11-12	Ps 119 (Vau)	Romans 7
May 5	Proverbs 5	I Samuel 13-14	Ps 119 (Zain)	Romans 8
May 6	Proverbs 6	I Samuel 15-16	Ps 119 (Cheth)	Romans 9
May 7	Proverbs 7	I Samuel 17-18	Ps 119 (Teth)	Romans 10
May 8	Proverbs 8	I Samuel 19-20	Ps 119 (Jod)	Romans 11
May 9	Proverbs 9	I Samuel 21-22	Ps 119 (Caph)	Romans 12
May 10	Proverbs 10	I Samuel 23-24	Ps 119 (Lamed)	Romans 13
May 11	Proverbs 11	I Samuel 25-26	Ps 119 (Mem)	Romans 14
May 12	Proverbs 12	I Samuel 27-28	Ps 119 (Nun)	Romans 15
May 13	Proverbs 13	I Samuel 29-30	Ps 119 (Samech)	Romans 16
May 14	Proverbs 14	I Samuel 31	Ps 119 (Ain)	I Corinthians 1
May 15	Proverbs 15	II Samuel 1-2	Ps 119 (Pe)	I Corinthians 2
May 16	Proverbs 16	II Samuel 3-4	Ps 119 (Tzaddi)	I Corinthians 3
May 17	Proverbs 17	II Samuel 5-6	Ps 119 (Koph)	I Corinthians 4
May 18	Proverbs 18	II Samuel 7-8	Ps 119 (Resh)	I Corinthians 5
May 19	Proverbs 19	II Samuel 9-10	Ps 119 (Schin)	I Corinthians 6
May 20	Proverbs 20	II Samuel 11-12	Ps 119 (Tau)	I Corinthians 7
May 21	Proverbs 21	II Samuel 13-14	Psalm 120	I Corinthians 8
May 22	Proverbs 22	II Samuel 15-16	Psalm 121	I Corinthians 9
May 23	Proverbs 23	II Samuel 17-18	Psalm 122	I Corinthians 10
May 24	Proverbs 24	II Samuel 19-20	Psalm 123	I Corinthians 11
May 25	Proverbs 25	II Samuel 21-22	Psalm 124	I Corinthians 12
May 26	Proverbs 26	II Samuel 23-24	Psalm 125	I Corinthians 13
May 27	Proverbs 27	I Kings 1-2	Psalm 126	I Corinthians 14
May 28	Proverbs 28	I Kings 3-4	Psalm 127	I Corinthians 15
May 29	Proverbs 29	I Kings 5-6	Psalm 128	I Corinthians 16
May 30	Proverbs 30	I Kings 7-8	Psalm 129	II Corinthians 1
May 31	Proverbs 31	I Kings 9-10	Psalm 130	II Corinthians 2

June

Date	Wisdom	Old Testament	Poetry	New Testament
June 1	Proverbs 1	I Kings 11-12	Psalm 131	II Corinthians 3
June 2	Proverbs 2	I Kings 13-14	Psalm 132	II Corinthians 4
June 3	Proverbs 3	I Kings 15-16	Psalm 133	II Corinthians 5
June 4	Proverbs 4	I Kings 17-18	Psalm 134	II Corinthians 6
June 5	Proverbs 5	I Kings 19-20	Psalm 135	II Corinthians 7
June 6	Proverbs 6	I Kings 21-22	Psalm 136	II Corinthians 8
June 7	Proverbs 7	II Kings 1-2	Psalm 137	II Corinthians 9
June 8	Proverbs 8	II Kings 3-4	Psalm 138	II Corinthians 10
June 9	Proverbs 9	II Kings 5-6	Psalm 139	II Corinthians 11
June 10	Proverbs 10	II Kings 7-8	Psalm 140	II Corinthians 12
June 11	Proverbs 11	II Kings 9-10	Psalm 141	II Corinthians 13
June 12	Proverbs 12	II Kings 11-12	Psalm 142	Galatians 1
June 13	Proverbs 13	II Kings 13-14	Psalm 143	Galatians 2
June 14	Proverbs 14	II Kings 15-16	Psalm 144	Galatians 3
June 15	Proverbs 15	II Kings 17-18	Psalm 145	Galatians 4
June 16	Proverbs 16	II Kings 19-20	Psalm 146	Galatians 5
June 17	Proverbs 17	II Kings 21-22	Psalm 147	Galatians 6
June 18	Proverbs 18	II Kings 23-24	Psalm 148	Ephesians 1
June 19	Proverbs 19	II Kings 25, I Chr. 1	Psalm 149	Ephesians 2
June 20	Proverbs 20	I Chronicles 2-3	Psalm 150	Ephesians 3
June 21	Proverbs 21	I Chronicles 4-5	Ecclesiastes 1	Ephesians 4
June 22	Proverbs 22	I Chronicles 6-7	Ecclesiastes 2	Ephesians 5
June 23	Proverbs 23	I Chronicles 8-9	Ecclesiastes 3	Ephesians 6
June 24	Proverbs 24	I Chronicles 10-11	Ecclesiastes 4	Philippians 1
June 25	Proverbs 25	I Chronicles 12-13	Ecclesiastes 5	Philippians 2
June 26	Proverbs 26	I Chronicles 14-15	Ecclesiastes 6	Philippians 3
June 27	Proverbs 27	I Chronicles 16-17	Ecclesiastes 7	Philippians 4
June 28	Proverbs 28	I Chronicles 18-19	Ecclesiastes 8	Colossians 1
June 29	Proverbs 29	I Chronicles 20-21	Ecclesiastes 9	Colossians 2
June 30	Proverbs 30	I Chronicles 22-23	Ecclesiastes 10	Colossians 3

July

Date	Wisdom	Old Testament	Poetry	New Testament
July 1	Proverbs 1	I Chronicles 24-25	Ecclesiastes 11	Colossians 4
July 2	Proverbs 2	I Chronicles 26-27	Ecclesiastes 12	I Thessalonians 1
July 3	Proverbs 3	I Chronicles 28-29	Psalm 1	I Thessalonians 2
July 4	Proverbs 4	II Chronicles 1-2	Psalm 2	I Thessalonians 3
July 5	Proverbs 5	II Chronicles 3-4	Psalm 3	I Thessalonians 4
July 6	Proverbs 6	II Chronicles 5-6	Psalm 4	I Thessalonians 5
July 7	Proverbs 7	II Chronicles 7-8	Psalm 5	II Thessalonians 1
July 8	Proverbs 8	II Chronicles 9-10	Psalm 6	II Thessalonians 2
July 9	Proverbs 9	II Chronicles 11-12	Psalm 7	II Thessalonians 3
July 10	Proverbs 10	II Chronicles 13-14	Psalm 8	Matthew 1
July 11	Proverbs 11	II Chronicles 15-16	Psalm 9	Matthew 2
July 12	Proverbs 12	II Chronicles 17-18	Psalm 10	Matthew 3
July 13	Proverbs 13	II Chronicles 19-20	Psalm 11	Matthew 4
July 14	Proverbs 14	II Chronicles 21-22	Psalm 12	Matthew 5
July 15	Proverbs 15	II Chronicles 23-24	Psalm 13	Matthew 6
July 16	Proverbs 16	II Chronicles 25-26	Psalm 14	Matthew 7
July 17	Proverbs 17	II Chronicles 27-28	Psalm 15	Matthew 8
July 18	Proverbs 18	II Chronicles 29-30	Psalm 16	Matthew 9
July 19	Proverbs 19	II Chronicles 31-32	Psalm 17	Matthew 10
July 20	Proverbs 20	II Chronicles 33-34	Psalm 18	Matthew 11
July 21	Proverbs 21	II Chronicles 35-36	Psalm 19	Matthew 12
July 22	Proverbs 22	Ezra 1-2	Psalm 20	Matthew 13
July 23	Proverbs 23	Ezra 3-4	Psalm 21	Matthew 14
July 24	Proverbs 24	Ezra 5-6	Psalm 22	Matthew 15
July 25	Proverbs 25	Ezra 7-8	Psalm 23	Matthew 16
July 26	Proverbs 26	Ezra 9-10	Psalm 24	Matthew 17
July 27	Proverbs 27	Nehemiah 1-2	Psalm 25	Matthew 18
July 28	Proverbs 28	Nehemiah 3-4	Psalm 26	Matthew 19
July 29	Proverbs 29	Nehemiah 5-6	Psalm 27	Matthew 20
July 30	Proverbs 30	Nehemiah 7-8	Psalm 28	Matthew 21
July 31	Proverbs 31	Nehemiah 9-10	Psalm 29	Matthew 22

August

Date	Wisdom	Old Testament	Poetry	New Testament
August 1	Proverbs 1	Nehemiah 11-13	Psalm 30	Matthew 23
August 2	Proverbs 2	Esther 1-2	Psalm 31	Matthew 24
August 3	Proverbs 3	Esther 3-4	Psalm 32	Matthew 25
August 4	Proverbs 4	Esther 5-6	Psalm 33	Matthew 26
August 5	Proverbs 5	Esther 7-8	Psalm 34	Matthew 27
August 6	Proverbs 6	Esther 9-10	Psalm 35	Matthew 28
August 7	Proverbs 7	Job 1-2	Psalm 36	Mark 1
August 8	Proverbs 8	Job 3-4	Psalm 37	Mark 2
August 9	Proverbs 9	Job 5-6	Psalm 38	Mark 3
August 10	Proverbs 10	Job 7-8	Psalm 39	Mark 4
August 11	Proverbs 11	Job 9-10	Psalm 40	Mark 5
August 12	Proverbs 12	Job 11-12	Psalm 41	Mark 6
August 13	Proverbs 13	Job 13-14	Psalm 42	Mark 7
August 14	Proverbs 14	Job 15-16	Psalm 43	Mark 8
August 15	Proverbs 15	Job 17-18	Psalm 44	Mark 9
August 16	Proverbs 16	Job 19-20	Psalm 45	Mark 10
August 17	Proverbs 17	Job 21-22	Psalm 46	Mark 11
August 18	Proverbs 18	Job 23-24	Psalm 47	Mark 12
August 19	Proverbs 19	Job 25-26	Psalm 48	Mark 13
August 20	Proverbs 20	Job 27-28	Psalm 49	Mark 14
August 21	Proverbs 21	Job 29-30	Psalm 50	Mark 15
August 22	Proverbs 22	Job 31-32	Psalm 51	Mark 16
August 23	Proverbs 23	Job 33-34	Psalm 52	Luke 1
August 24	Proverbs 24	Job 35-36	Psalm 53	Luke 2
August 25	Proverbs 25	Job 37-38	Psalm 54	Luke 3
August 26	Proverbs 26	Job 39-40	Psalm 55	Luke 4
August 27	Proverbs 27	Job 41-42	Psalm 56	Luke 5
August 28	Proverbs 28	Song of Songs 1-2	Psalm 57	Luke 6
August 29	Proverbs 29	Song of Songs 3-4	Psalm 58	Luke 7
August 30	Proverbs 30	Song of Songs 5-6	Psalm 59	Luke 8
August 31	Proverbs 31	Song of Songs 7-8	Psalm 60	Luke 9

September

Devotional Bible Reading

Date	Wisdom	Old Testament	Poetry	New Testament
September 1	Proverbs 1	Isaiah 1-2	Psalm 61	Luke 10
September 2	Proverbs 2	Isaiah 3-4	Psalm 62	Luke 11
September 3	Proverbs 3	Isaiah 5-6	Psalm 63	Luke 12
September 4	Proverbs 4	Isaiah 7-8	Psalm 64	Luke 13
September 5	Proverbs 5	Isaiah 9-10	Psalm 65	Luke 14
September 6	Proverbs 6	Isaiah 11-12	Psalm 66	Luke 15
September 7	Proverbs 7	Isaiah 13-14	Psalm 67	Luke 16
September 8	Proverbs 8	Isaiah 15-16	Psalm 68	Luke 17
September 9	Proverbs 9	Isaiah 17-18	Psalm 69	Luke 18
September 10	Proverbs 10	Isaiah 19-20	Psalm 70	Luke 19
September 11	Proverbs 11	Isaiah 21-22	Psalm 71	Luke 20
September 12	Proverbs 12	Isaiah 23-24	Psalm 72	Luke 21
September 13	Proverbs 13	Isaiah 25-26	Psalm 73	Luke 22
September 14	Proverbs 14	Isaiah 27-28	Psalm 74	Luke 23
September 15	Proverbs 15	Isaiah 29-30	Psalm 75	Luke 24
September 16	Proverbs 16	Isaiah 31-32	Psalm 76	John 1
September 17	Proverbs 17	Isaiah 33-34	Psalm 77	John 2
September 18	Proverbs 18	Isaiah 35-36	Psalm 78	John 3
September 19	Proverbs 19	Isaiah 37-38	Psalm 79	John 4
September 20	Proverbs 20	Isaiah 39-40	Psalm 80	John 5
September 21	Proverbs 21	Isaiah 41-42	Psalm 81	John 6
September 22	Proverbs 22	Isaiah 43-44	Psalm 82	John 7
September 23	Proverbs 23	Isaiah 45-46	Psalm 83	John 8
September 24	Proverbs 24	Isaiah 47-48	Psalm 84	John 9
September 25	Proverbs 25	Isaiah 49-50	Psalm 85	John 10
September 26	Proverbs 26	Isaiah 51-52	Psalm 86	John 11
September 27	Proverbs 27	Isaiah 53-54	Psalm 87	John 12
September 28	Proverbs 28	Isaiah 55-56	Psalm 88	John 13
September 29	Proverbs 29	Isaiah 57-58	Psalm 89	John 14
September 30	Proverbs 30	Isaiah 59-60	Psalm 90	John 15

Page 13

October

Date	Wisdom	Old Testament	Poetry	New Testament
October 1	Proverbs 1	Isaiah 61-62	Psalm 91	John 16
October 2	Proverbs 2	Isaiah 63-64	Psalm 92	John 17
October 3	Proverbs 3	Isaiah 65-66	Psalm 93	John 18
October 4	Proverbs 4	Jeremiah 1-2	Psalm 94	John 19
October 5	Proverbs 5	Jeremiah 3-4	Psalm 95	John 20
October 6	Proverbs 6	Jeremiah 5-6	Psalm 96	John 21
October 7	Proverbs 7	Jeremiah 7-8	Psalm 97	Romans 1
October 8	Proverbs 8	Jeremiah 9-10	Psalm 98	Romans 2
October 9	Proverbs 9	Jeremiah 11-12	Psalm 99	Romans 3
October 10	Proverbs 10	Jeremiah 13-14	Psalm 100	Romans 4
October 11	Proverbs 11	Jeremiah 15-16	Psalm 101	Romans 5
October 12	Proverbs 12	Jeremiah 17-18	Psalm 102	Romans 6
October 13	Proverbs 13	Jeremiah 19-20	Psalm 103	Romans 7
October 14	Proverbs 14	Jeremiah 21-22	Psalm 104	Romans 8
October 15	Proverbs 15	Jeremiah 23-24	Psalm 105	Romans 9
October 16	Proverbs 16	Jeremiah 25-26	Psalm 106	Romans 10
October 17	Proverbs 17	Jeremiah 27-28	Psalm 107	Romans 11
October 18	Proverbs 18	Jeremiah 29-30	Psalm 108	Romans 12
October 19	Proverbs 19	Jeremiah 31-32	Psalm 109	Romans 13
October 20	Proverbs 20	Jeremiah 33-34	Psalm 110	Romans 14
October 21	Proverbs 21	Jeremiah 35-36	Psalm 111	Romans 15
October 22	Proverbs 22	Jeremiah 37-38	Psalm 112	Romans 16
October 23	Proverbs 23	Jeremiah 39-40	Psalm 113	I Timothy 1
October 24	Proverbs 24	Jeremiah 41-42	Psalm 114	I Timothy 2
October 25	Proverbs 25	Jeremiah 43-44	Psalm 115	I Timothy 3
October 26	Proverbs 26	Jeremiah 45-46	Ps 116 & 117	I Timothy 4
October 27	Proverbs 27	Jeremiah 47-48	Psalm 118	I Timothy 5
October 28	Proverbs 28	Jeremiah 49-50	Ps 119 (Aleph)	I Timothy 6
October 29	Proverbs 29	Jeremiah 51-52	Ps 119 (Beth)	II Timothy 1
October 30	Proverbs 30	Lamentations 1-2	Ps 119 (Gimel)	II Timothy 2
October 31	Proverbs 31	Lamentations 3-5	Ps 119 (Daleth)	II Timothy 3

November

Date	Wisdom	Old Testament	Poetry	New Testament
November 1	Proverbs 1	Ezekiel 1-2	Ps 119 (He)	II Timothy 4
November 2	Proverbs 2	Ezekiel 3-4	Ps 119 (Vau)	Titus 1
November 3	Proverbs 3	Ezekiel 5-6	Ps 119 (Zain)	Titus 2
November 4	Proverbs 4	Ezekiel 7-8	Ps 119 (Cheth)	Titus 3
November 5	Proverbs 5	Ezekiel 9-10	Ps 119 (Teth)	Philemon
November 6	Proverbs 6	Ezekiel 11-12	Ps 119 (Jod)	Hebrews 1
November 7	Proverbs 7	Ezekiel 13-14	Ps 119 (Caph)	Hebrews 2
November 8	Proverbs 8	Ezekiel 15-16	Ps 119 (Lamed)	Hebrews 3
November 9	Proverbs 9	Ezekiel 17-18	Ps 119 (Mem)	Hebrews 4
November 10	Proverbs 10	Ezekiel 19-20	Ps 119 (Nun)	Hebrews 5
November 11	Proverbs 11	Ezekiel 21-22	Ps 119 (Samech)	Hebrews 6
November 12	Proverbs 12	Ezekiel 23-24	Ps 119 (Ain)	Hebrews 7
November 13	Proverbs 13	Ezekiel 25-26	Ps 119 (Pe)	Hebrews 8
November 14	Proverbs 14	Ezekiel 27-28	Ps 119 (Tzaddi)	Hebrews 9
November 15	Proverbs 15	Ezekiel 29-30	Ps 119 (Koph)	Hebrews 10
November 16	Proverbs 16	Ezekiel 31-32	Ps 119 (Resh)	Hebrews 11
November 17	Proverbs 17	Ezekiel 33-34	Ps 119 (Schin)	Hebrews 12
November 18	Proverbs 18	Ezekiel 35-36	Ps 119 (Tau)	Hebrews 13
November 19	Proverbs 19	Ezekiel 37-38	Psalm 120	James 1
November 20	Proverbs 20	Ezekiel 39-40	Psalm 121	James 2
November 21	Proverbs 21	Ezekiel 41-42	Psalm 122	James 3
November 22	Proverbs 22	Ezekiel 43-44	Psalm 123	James 4
November 23	Proverbs 23	Ezekiel 45-46	Psalm 124	James 5
November 24	Proverbs 24	Ezekiel 47-48	Psalm 125	I Peter 1
November 25	Proverbs 25	Daniel 1-2	Psalm 126	I Peter 2
November 26	Proverbs 26	Daniel 3-4	Psalm 127	I Peter 3
November 27	Proverbs 27	Daniel 5-6	Psalm 128	I Peter 4
November 28	Proverbs 28	Daniel 7-8	Psalm 129	I Peter 5
November 29	Proverbs 29	Daniel 9-10	Psalm 130	II Peter 1
November 30	Proverbs 30	Daniel 11-12	Psalm 131	II Peter 2

December

Date	Wisdom	Old Testament	Poetry	New Testament
December 1	Proverbs 1	Hosea 1-2	Psalm 132	II Peter 3
December 2	Proverbs 2	Hosea 3-4	Psalm 133	I John 1
December 3	Proverbs 3	Hosea 5-6	Psalm 134	I John 2
December 4	Proverbs 4	Hosea 7-8	Psalm 135	I John 3
December 5	Proverbs 5	Hosea 9-10	Psalm 136	I John 4
December 6	Proverbs 6	Hosea 11-12	Psalm 137	I John 5
December 7	Proverbs 7	Hosea 13-14	Psalm 138	II John
December 8	Proverbs 8	Joel 1-3	Psalm 139	III John
December 9	Proverbs 9	Amos 1-2	Psalm 140	Jude
December 10	Proverbs 10	Amos 3-4	Psalm 141	Revelation 1
December 11	Proverbs 11	Amos 5-6	Psalm 142	Revelation 2
December 12	Proverbs 12	Amos 7-8	Psalm 143	Revelation 3
December 13	Proverbs 13	Amos 9, Obadiah	Psalm 144	Revelation 4
December 14	Proverbs 14	Jonah 1-2	Psalm 145	Revelation 5
December 15	Proverbs 15	Jonah 3-4	Psalm 146	Revelation 6
December 16	Proverbs 16	Micah 1-2	Psalm 147	Revelation 7
December 17	Proverbs 17	Micah 3-4	Psalm 148	Revelation 8
December 18	Proverbs 18	Micah 5-7	Psalm 149	Revelation 9
December 19	Proverbs 19	Nahum 1-3	Psalm 150	Revelation 10
December 20	Proverbs 20	Habakkuk 1-3	Ecclesiastes 1	Revelation 11
December 21	Proverbs 21	Zephaniah 1-3	Ecclesiastes 2	Revelation 12
December 22	Proverbs 22	Haggai 1-2	Ecclesiastes 3	Revelation 13
December 23	Proverbs 23	Zechariah 1-2	Ecclesiastes 4	Revelation 14
December 24	Proverbs 24	Zechariah 3-4	Ecclesiastes 5	Revelation 15
December 25	Proverbs 25	Zechariah 5-6	Ecclesiastes 6	Revelation 16
December 26	Proverbs 26	Zechariah 7-8	Ecclesiastes 7	Revelation 17
December 27	Proverbs 27	Zechariah 9-10	Ecclesiastes 8	Revelation 18
December 28	Proverbs 28	Zechariah 11-12	Ecclesiastes 9	Revelation 19
December 29	Proverbs 29	Zechariah 13-14	Ecclesiastes 10	Revelation 20
December 30	Proverbs 30	Malachi 1-2	Ecclesiastes 11	Revelation 21
December 31	Proverbs 31	Malachi 3-4	Ecclesiastes 12	Revelation 22

Chapter 2

Survey Studies

Study and be eager and do your utmost to present yourself to God approved (tested by trial), a workman who has no cause to be ashamed, correctly analyzing and accurately dividing [rightly handling and skillfully teaching] the Word of Truth.
- 2 Timothy 2:15 (AMP)

A survey study is an overview of the entire Bible or a significant portion of the Bible, such as the Old Testament or the New Testament. It makes use of external sources to conduct the survey, so it is more a study OF the Bible than it is a study FROM the Bible.

Two good survey studies for the Old Testament are *Exploring the Old Testament* by W.T. Purkiser, and the *Old Testament Speaks* by Samuel J. Schultz. For the New Testament, I suggest *New Testament Survey* by Merrill C. Tenney, or *New Testament Survey* by Robert G. Gromacki.

Here is a brief Bible survey, taken from chapter two of *How To Study Your Bible:*

Old Testament

The Pentateuch – Genesis, Exodus, Leviticus, Numbers, and Deuteronomy

Pentateuch (pronounced *pent-uh-tewk*) means "five books," and these make up the opening section of the Old Testament. Moses was the author of these books, which contain the origins of creation and the 12 tribes of Israel, as well as details about the Law God gave to Moses for the Israelites to follow.

Historical Books – Joshua, Judges, Ruth, 1 Samuel, 2 Samuel, 1 Kings, 2 Kings, 1 Chronicles, 2 Chronicles, Ezra, Nehemiah, and Esther

These books, written by various authors, continue to tell the story of the nation of Israel. Joshua, Judges, and Ruth cover the conquest of the land of Canaan and the history of the twelve tribes of Israel before the monarchy. First and Second Samuel tell the story of how Israel became a nation ruled by a king.

First and Second Kings cover the dividing of the kingdom into two opposing nations, Israel and Judah, and the reigns of the kings that followed in each nation, up until the captivity period. First and Second Chronicles cover much of the same material related in First and Second Kings, but First and Second Kings tell the story from the Kingdom of Israel's point of view, while First and Second Chronicles cover it from the viewpoint of the Kingdom of Judah.

Eventually, both the Kingdoms of Israel and of Judah fell due to their sin. Israel was conquered by the nation of Assyria, and Judah fell to the armies of Babylon. At that time it was the practice of these nations to carry the populations of the people they conquered into captivity. The books of Ezra, Nehemiah, and Esther reflect the period of the Judean captivity in Babylon and their eventual return to the land of Israel when their captivity was over.

Poetry Books – Job, Psalms, Proverbs, Ecclesiastes, and Song of Solomon

Sometimes referred to as the Wisdom books, this group represents writings that are more poetic in nature. The story of Job is considered to be one of the oldest writings in the world. Psalms contains the lyrics of songs, mostly written by King David, but some were also written by Moses and others. Proverbs, Ecclesiastes, and Song of Solomon were written by King David's son, King Solomon, who is considered the wisest man in the history of the world.

Major Prophets – Isaiah, Jeremiah, Lamentations, Ezekiel, and Daniel

The Prophets were God's spokesmen in the Old Testament. They were the ones who said, "Thus saith the Lord," delivering the messages God had for His people. The writings included in the Major Prophets are of greater length than those of the Minor Prophets, and also cover subjects and events that are of generally greater importance. Each book is named after its author, with Jeremiah also having written Lamentations.

Minor Prophets – Hosea, Joel, Amos, Obadiah, Jonah, Micah, Nahum, Habakkuk, Zephaniah, Haggai, Zechariah, and Malachi

The Minor Prophets, sometimes referred to as the Book of the Twelve because there are 12 of them, are similar to the writings of the Major Prophets, but they are typically much shorter. These are the pages that are usually stuck together in the back of your Old Testament. The last of the Minor Prophets was the Book of Malachi, after which there was over 400 years of silence as history passed, until the time the next books of the Bible were written.

New Testament

The Gospels – Matthew, Mark, Luke, and John

The four Gospels tell the good news of the birth, life, and ministry of the Lord Jesus Christ, climaxing with His death on the cross, His burial, and His resurrection. Technically speaking, Jesus operated on Earth as a Prophet under the Old Covenant.

Therefore, it could be argued, from a theological standpoint, that the Gospels should be grouped with the Old Testament, since the New Covenant didn't actually begin until after Jesus' resurrection. However, since they are historically closer to the rest of the New Testament books, they make up the opening books of the New Testament.

History – Acts

The Book of Acts details the history of the Apostles and the growth of the early church in the years immediately following the ministry of Jesus. The first twelve chapters emphasize the ministry of the Apostle Peter, while the remaining sixteen chapters focus on the ministry of the Apostle Paul, especially his missionary journeys throughout the Roman Empire.

Pauline Epistles – Romans, 1 and 2 Corinthians, Galatians, Ephesians, Philippians, Colossians, 1 and 2 Thessalonians, 1 and 2 Timothy, Titus, and Philemon

The word "epistle" means a formal letter, and this group of books consists of letters written by the Apostle Paul. The Pauline Epistles can be subdivided into two groups: letters to churches and Pastoral Epistles. The churches that Paul wrote to were those he started or visited during his missionary trips, detailed in the Book of Acts. For example, the Book of Ephesians was written to the church at Ephesus. The Pastoral Epistles were written to individuals. Timothy and Titus were ministers that Paul mentored, and Philemon was one of his supporters.

General Epistles – Hebrews, James, 1 Peter, 2 Peter, 1 John, 2 John, 3 John, and Jude

The General Epistles are so named because they were written to the entire church in general. The Pauline Epistles were always specifically addressed either to a certain church or to an individual, but the General Epistles were written to the church at large. Except for the Book of Hebrews, the General Epistles are named after their authors, the Apostles Peter and John, and also James and Jude, who were two of Jesus' younger brothers.

It isn't 100% clear who wrote the Book of Hebrews, as the author isn't identified. However, most believe it was probably either Paul, or someone who worked closely with Paul, and the Book of Hebrews should be grouped with the Pauline Epistles (as it was historically). Like the other General Epistles, it was written to all of the Hebrew Christians who were spread out across the Roman Empire.

Prophecy - Revelation

The only prophetic writing of the New Testament, the Book of Revelation, covers God's judgment upon those who rejected His Son, along with the events that will happen at the end of the age. It ends on an encouraging note with the final defeat of God's enemies and the revelation of a new Heaven and Earth.

Final Thoughts on Survey Studies

Think of a survey study as a 10,000-foot high view of the Bible. You probably won't pick up a lot of details from the survey itself, but once you have an idea of the overall layout of the map, it becomes much easier to go to a certain place on that map so you can see things close up and in greater detail.

You do have to keep in mind that surveys of the Old and New Testaments are written by men, and sometimes their thoughts and opinions will seep into the content. The Bible is inspired by the Holy Spirit, but books written about the Bible are not. This is always something you should keep in mind when reading books about the Bible. However, the general nature of survey studies makes it much less likely that false doctrines will be a problem.

In other words, because survey studies simply cover the broad outlines and structure of the Bible, you don't have to be as concerned about their authenticity as you do with other Bible study tools. You can find many good survey study books online. Just be aware of any possible doctrinal biases or agendas on the part of the author.

EXERCISE 2-1

Tools Needed: *Your Bible, a pencil, a notebook, and a Bible survey study resource*

Find a Bible survey study resource, either online, at your local library, or purchase one. Read the survey material about a part of the Bible that you're interested in. Use your notebook to write down any new information you discover. Save your survey notes for future use.

EXERCISE 2-2

Tools Needed: *Your Bible, a pencil, Sword Drills workbook*

Complete the following:

A) Put these books of the Bible in order:

1) _____   Exodus

2) _____   Deuteronomy

3) _____   Numbers

4) _____   Genesis

5) _____   Leviticus

What section of the Bible are these books from?

_____

B) Put these books of the Bible in order:

1) _____   Song of Solomon

2) _____   Psalms

3) _____   Ecclesiastes

4) _____   Job

5) _____   Proverbs

What section of the Bible are these books from?

_____

C) Put these books of the Bible in order:

1) _____   Jeremiah

2) _____   Daniel

3) _____   Isaiah

4) _____   Lamentations

5) _____   Ezekiel

What section of the Bible are these books from?

_____

D) Put these books of the Bible in order:

1) _____   Acts

2) _____   Matthew

3) _____   John

4) _____   Luke

5) _____   Mark

What section of the Bible are these books from?

_____

E) Put these books of the Bible in order:

1) _____	Colossians
2) _____	Ephesians
3) _____	Romans
4) _____	Galatians
5) _____	Philippians

What section of the Bible are these books from?

_____

F) Put these books of the Bible in order:

1) _____	James
2) _____	1 John
3) _____	2 Peter
4) _____	Jude
5) _____	3 John

What section of the Bible are these books from?

_____

G) Put these SECTIONS of the Bible in order:

1) _____	Historical Books
2) _____	Major Prophets
3) _____	Minor Prophets
4) _____	Pentateuch
5) _____	Poetry Books

What Testament of the Bible are these from?

_____

H) Put these SECTIONS of the Bible in order:

1) _____	Pauline Epistles
2) _____	History
3) _____	General Epistles
4) _____	Gospels
5) _____	Prophecy

What Testament of the Bible are these from?

_____

I) Fill in the blanks:

1) Joshua, _____, Ruth

2) Ezra, Nehemiah, _____

3) 1 Samuel, 2 Samuel, _____

4) Amos, _____, Jonah

J) Draw lines connecting the names of the Minor Prophets in order:

Hosea	Malachi	Zechariah	Haggai
Joel	Jonah	Micah	Zephaniah
Amos	Obadiah	Nahum	Habakkuk

K) Fill in the blanks:

1) _____, Titus, Philemon   3) Mark, Luke, _____

2) Hebrews, James, _____   4) Galatians, _____, Philippians

L) Draw lines connecting the names of the Pauline Epistles in order:

Romans	1 Corinthians	Titus	2 Timothy
Galatians	2 Corinthians	Philemon	1 Timothy
Ephesians	Colossians	1 Thessalonians	2 Thessalonians
Philippians			

M) Answer the following questions:

1) Which book is NOT one of the four Gospels?

    a) Matthew   b) James   c) Luke   d) John

2) Which of the books listed below appears first in the Bible before the other three?

    a) Job   b) Hosea   c) Acts   d) Jude

3) Which book is NOT one of the Major Prophets?

    a) Ezekiel   b) Isaiah   c) Jeremiah   d) Zechariah

4) Which spelling is correct?

    a) Revelations   b) Revolution   c) Revelation   d) Revealitions

Note: Go to the Answer Key on page 65 to check your answers

Chapter 3
Word Studies

To whom will he teach knowledge, and to whom will he explain the message?
Those who are weaned from the milk, those taken from the breast?
For it is precept upon precept, precept upon precept,
line upon line, line upon line, here a little, there a little. – Isaiah 28:9, 10

While the survey study gives you a great bird's-eye view, the word study zooms all the way in to literally focus on a single word. Not only is it exciting to uncover new Bible truths through a word study, but this Bible study method is the foundation for all of the other study methods that will follow.

A common misconception of word studies is that they are studies of words that appear in the English version of the Bible. A word study is not a study of the English word, but rather it's a study of that word in the original language. Put differently, a word study is actually the study of how a particular Hebrew or Greek word is used in the Bible.

(Note: This chapter assumes you already have a working knowledge of how to use a Strong's Exhaustive Concordance of the Bible. If you don't, you can learn more in chapter 3 of *How To Study Your Bible.)*

Steps to Perform a Word Study

Step 1 – Decide what word you want to study

This part is pretty easy. Maybe you heard a preacher say something in a message that piqued your curiosity and you want to follow up, or perhaps you have a question about what a certain verse means. When you're hungry for the things of God, it's not hard to come up with a whole list of things you'd like to learn more about. The most challenging aspect of this step is narrowing your word list down to just one single word.

Step 2 – See how often the word is used in Scripture

Look up the word in your concordance and see if it's a word that's used hundreds of times or just a few times. If it's a word that's used a lot in the Bible, you may be looking at a more in-depth study. On the other hand, the frequency with which a word is used can also give insights. For example, a word study on the word "faith" would probably be more worthwhile than one on the word "dragons."

As one pastor put it, "We should major on the majors, and minor on the minors." In other words, we should be spending the majority of our study time on things the Bible emphasizes, and less time on things the Bible mentions less frequently.

Step 3 – Identify the Strong's number for that word

This step is also easy. Look up the word in Strong's and find the reference number. For example, if I wanted to study the word "faith" in the New Testament, I would find that the Strong's number is G4102.

Step 4 – Look up the Greek or Hebrew word

Next, look the word up in the Hebrew or Greek dictionary, whichever applies. Following our example, I would find that G4102 is the Greek word *pistis,* along with the definition. I would also discover that *pistis* is translated into the English words "assurance, belief, believe, faith, and fidelity."

Step 5 – Use other research tools to gain further insights

Once again, the Greek and Hebrew dictionaries found at the back of Strong's Concordance are very basic. In order to gain a more complete understanding of the word, it may be useful to consult other research tools, such as *Vine's Expository Dictionary of New Testament Words* or a lexical study Bible.

Following Up

At this point I have a decision to make. If I am just looking for a quick definition, then I'm done. However, if I want to do an in-depth study on the subject of faith, there are many, many verses containing the word *pistis,* which indicates to me that this particular study will take a significant amount of time. In-depth word studies are actually the first building block of many other Bible study methods, which is why we are covering them first before moving on to those other methods.

EXERCISE 3-1

Tools Needed: Your Bible, Strong's Concordance, Sword Drills workbook or notebook

Complete the following:

A) Using your Concordance, find the verse:

1) Where does the Bible say that God loves a cheerful giver?　　　　＿＿＿＿＿＿＿＿＿＿

2) Where does the Bible say not to touch God's anointed one?　　　　＿＿＿＿＿＿＿＿＿＿

3) Where does the Bible say that the eyes are the window to the soul?　　＿＿＿＿＿＿＿＿＿＿

B) What are the four main sections of Strong's Concordance?

1) ＿＿＿＿＿＿＿＿＿＿＿＿＿＿＿＿＿＿＿＿

2) ＿＿＿＿＿＿＿＿＿＿＿＿＿＿＿＿＿＿＿＿

3) ＿＿＿＿＿＿＿＿＿＿＿＿＿＿＿＿＿＿＿＿

4) ＿＿＿＿＿＿＿＿＿＿＿＿＿＿＿＿＿＿＿＿

Note: Go to the Answer Key on page 65 to check your answers

C) Using your Concordance, do this word study on "praise"

1) How many Hebrew words for "praise" are in the Old Testament? _____

2) What are they? _____

3) What is the general definition of each of these words? (Use space below for your answer)

Note: Go to the Answer Key on page 65 to check your answers

EXERCISE 3-2

Tools Needed: *Your Bible, Strong's Concordance, Sword Drills workbook or notebook*

During your daily devotional reading, you come across this verse:

> *He also that received seed among the thorns is he that heareth the word; <u>and the care of this world</u>, and the deceitfulness of riches, choke the word, and he becometh unfruitful. - Matthew 13:22*

(Note: for purposes of this illustration we will be using the King James Version.) You wonder what is meant by the phrase "cares of the world," and so you decide to do a word study on the word translated as "care."

Complete the following:

Look up "care" in your Strong's Concordance, and find the line referencing Matthew 13:22.

1) The word translated "cares" was originally written in what language?

    a) Hebrew   b) Greek

2) How do you know the word was originally written in that language?

_____

3) What is the Strong's number for that word? _____

Look up that Strong's number in the relevant dictionary in the back of the Concordance.

4) What is the original Greek word that was translated as "care?" _____

5) What other English words are translated from that Greek word? _____

6) Are there any other words that are similar to that Greek word? _____

7) If so, what are they? _____

8) What other English words are translated from the additional Greek words, if any?

_____

At this point you should have identified G3308 and G3309 as the related Greek words translated as "care" in English. For further study you could look up all of those English words in your Strong's Concordance: *care, careful, take.*

For further insights, you could consult *Vine's Expository Dictionary of New Testament Words* or a lexical study Bible. We will return to this particular word study when we look at topical studies in chapter 5.

EXERCISE 3-3

Tools Needed: *Your Bible, Strong's Concordance, notebook*

Once there was a preacher who wanted to know the difference between the Holy Spirit and the Holy Ghost. He looked up references to both phrases and listed each of them out. Next, he made a list of similarities and differences between the two. Finally, he made a discovery that resolved the question for him once and for all.

A) How would you duplicate the steps of his word study if you were doing it?

B) What do you think the discovery he made at the end was?

EXERCISE 3-4

Tools Needed: *Your Bible, Strong's Concordance, notebook*

"Sorcery" is strictly forbidden in the Bible. Do a word study of the word "sorceries" and see what you discover.

A) If you aren't a Satanist or part of some spiritual fringe group, is sorcery relevant to you?

Note: Go to the Answer Key on page 65 to check your answers

Congratulations! You now know how to perform a word study. This is how word studies are done. It's real mental work and it isn't glamorous, but some of the insights you will stumble upon and some of the connections you make while doing word studies will be extremely exciting, and that will make all of your efforts worth it.

Chapter 4
Verse Studies

So Philip ran to him and heard him reading Isaiah the prophet and asked, "Do you understand what you are reading?" – Acts 8:30

A verse study is performed to enable you to understand the meaning of a particular verse or verses, and to answer the questions, "What does this verse mean? What does it teach me?"

Steps to Perform a Verse Study

Step 1 – Identify the source of the verse

Imagine reading a magazine containing both news stories and poems. You would read the poetry differently than you would the prose of the news story because they are two different kinds of literature. Be aware of the book and book division of the Bible where the Scripture passage is found. This will help you interpret which type of literature the verse is and how it should be read.

Step 2 – Read the entire chapter

Read the entire chapter where the Scripture passage appears. Take special note of the verses before and after your specific verse. This will help you see the correct context of the verse.

Step 3 – Pray about the verse

Ask the Lord to teach you by His Spirit, "What does this verse teach? What is the practical application of it for me today?" Do this before looking at any outside study materials, because those might give you preconceived ideas which could cause you to miss the voice of the Spirit.

Step 4 – Research the verse

To help you better understand the verse, use Bible study tools such as Bible dictionaries, a concordance, commentaries, and Hebrew/Greek word studies. I'm sure it's already clear to you how a parallel Bible or a good study Bible can be of great benefit in helping you understand the meaning of a verse.

Step 5 – Analyze the verse

This is the key step. All of the other steps lead up to this one: Read through the verse and write down notes about anything you see within the verse.

Now read it a second time. Every time you see something new that the verse teaches, write it down. "This verse teaches _____." Repeat this process at least 10 times, reading the verse and writing down what it teaches. Double that would be better, but when you're getting started, it's hard to see as much as you'll be able to after you've been doing it for a while.

The Word of God is literally inexhaustible. There will always be new nuggets of insight you can mine from a verse, no matter how many times you've looked at it before. It will amaze you how much you'll find in a single verse, in just one sitting, each time you go through it again for this exercise.

Exercise 4-1

Tools Needed: *Your Bible, Sword Drills workbook or notebook*

First, Read 1 Peter 1:1, 2

> *1 Peter, an apostle of Jesus Christ, to the strangers scattered throughout Pontus, Galatia, Cappadocia, Asia, and Bithynia,*
>
> *2 Elect according to the foreknowledge of God the Father, through sanctification of the Spirit, unto obedience and sprinkling of the blood of Jesus Christ: Grace unto you, and peace, be multiplied.*

Next, perform a verse study on those two verses, following the steps listed on page 27.

When you're finished, write "This verse teaches me _____." Make a listing of every single thing you find as you analyze these two verses.

Try to pull absolutely everything you can out of these two verses, and write them down in the space below. When you're finished, turn the page and compare your list with my list.

Verse study of 1 Peter 1:1, 2 - by Michael Dorsey

> *1 Peter, an apostle of Jesus Christ, to the strangers scattered throughout Pontus, Galatia, Cappadocia, Asia, and Bithynia,*
>
> *2 Elect according to the foreknowledge of God the Father, through sanctification of the Spirit, unto obedience and sprinkling of the blood of Jesus Christ: Grace unto you, and peace, be multiplied.*

These verses teach:

1) This epistle is by Peter

2) This Peter who wrote this epistle was an apostle of Jesus Christ

3) Peter delighted to think and speak of himself as one sent of Jesus Christ (compare 2 Pet. 1:1)

4) The name "Jesus Christ" is used twice in these 2 verses. Significance:

    a) Savior

    b) Anointed One

    c) Fulfiller of the Messianic predictions of the Old Testament "Christ." It especially has reference to the earthly ministry of Christ.

5) This epistle was written to the elect, especially to the elect who are sojourners of the dispersion in Pontus.

6) Believers are:

    a) Elect or chosen of God

    b) Foreknown of God

    c) Sanctified by the Spirit

    d) Sprinkled by the blood of Jesus Christ

    e) Sojourners or pilgrims on the Earth

    f) Subjects of multiplied grace

    g) Possessors of multiplied peace

7) Election:

    a) Who are the elect? Believers (compare 1 Peter 1:5)

    b) To what are they elected?

        i) Obedience

        ii) Sprinkling of the blood of Jesus

    c) According to what are they elect? The fore-knowledge of God

d) In what are they elect? Sanctification of the Spirit

e) The test of election: Obedience

f) The work of the three Persons of the Trinity in election are:

    i) The Father foreknows

    ii) Jesus Christ cleanses from guilt by His blood

    ii) The Spirit sanctifies

8) God is the Father of the elect

9) The humanity of Christ: seen in the mention of His blood

10) The reality of the body of Jesus Christ: seen in the mention of His blood

11) It is by His blood and not by his example that Jesus delivers from sin

12) Peter's first and greatest wish and prayer for those to whom he wrote was that grace and peace might be multiplied

13) It is not enough to have grace and peace. One should have multiplied grace and peace

14) That men already have grace and peace is no reason to cease praying for them, but rather it is an incentive to prayer that they may have more grace and peace

15) Grace comes <u>before</u> peace

Now, when you did the exercise, you probably didn't get anywhere near as much out of First Peter 1:1, 2 as I did. That's okay! Do NOT be discouraged! This is not a competition. My purpose for this exercise wasn't to show off how "Bible smart" I am, but to illustrate just HOW MUCH insight and revelation can be pulled from only a couple of Bible verses.

I'm sure if I come back to these verses a year from now, I will see something new that I didn't see this time around. Let this be an encouragement for you to really dig into the Word when you do a verse study. Don't EVER think you've pulled everything out of a verse, because there is always more light and truth to be found.

Chapter 5
Topical Studies

But all things should be done decently and in order. - 1 Corinthians 14:40

A topical study is an in-depth study of a particular Bible topic, either through a single book, the Old or New Testament, or the entire Bible. The subject of your topical study can be almost anything you can think of that's in the Bible. The Topical Method is important for these reasons:

1) It enables us to study the Word of God systematically, logically, and in an orderly manner.

2) It gives us a proper perspective and balance regarding biblical truth. We get to see the whole of a biblical teaching.

3) It allows us to study subjects that are of particular interest to us.

4) It enables us to study the great doctrines of the Bible.

5) It lends itself to good and lively discussions. The results of a topical study are always easy to share with others.

6) It allows us variety in our personal Bible study.

All topical studies begin as word studies, but they can turn into massive verse studies, so proficiency in both of these Bible study methods will serve you well with topical studies. Once you have a topic you want to study, make a list of questions you have about that topic.

Steps to Perform a Topical Study

Step 1 – Find the Strong's reference number for the word

If I wanted to do an in-depth study on faith in the New Testament, the first thing I would do is look it up in Strong's Concordance, where I would find that it is the word *pistis* in Greek (G4202).

Step 2 – Find all the Bible verses using that word

Next I would look up all the English words translated from that word and make a list of all the Bible verses that contain the word *pistis* (G4202), either by typing them out or copying them onto a document on the computer. Typing them by hand is a good way to ingrain each verse in your mind, but if it's a word like *pistis* that has a lot of entries, this may not be practical.

Step 3 – Analyze each verse

Using the Verse Study method, make some notes about what you find in each verse. It can be helpful at this stage to write each verse on an index card. This step may take some time if there are a lot of verses related to your topic, but don't be lazy. It's very important that your verse analysis is thorough.

Step 4 – Sort the verses

Categorize verses that naturally complement each other and group them together on a separate sheet of paper. If you are using index cards as suggested, you can simply move the verse cards around into their appropriate groups. Larger sticky notes are also good to use for this step.

Step 5 – Define your sub-topics

Using each category as a subject heading, logically arrange the groups of Scriptures into an outline. This will make it easier for you to remember and will also make it easier for you to communicate to others what you've learned.

Step 6 – Consult reference materials

At this point you've squeezed all you can out of these verses, so check the topical Bible study tools mentioned in this chapter to look for any further insights. It's always best to do your own analysis before consulting any reference materials. Even if you find something that's already covered in those books, the exercise of discovering it on your own will be more helpful to your Bible study career over the long term.

Step 7 – Apply what you've learned

Conclude your study with a practical application you can put to use in your own life. Write a brief paragraph summary of what you discovered in your topical study, and list the ways you can immediately apply your findings to your daily life.

Following Up

Due to the way Bible verses are sorted out in a topical study, it can be very easy to take things out of context, so be systematic. Don't try to study the Bible in a haphazard, undisciplined manner. When you make your list of the things related to your topic, make it as comprehensive and complete as possible. Then take up these sub-topics one at a time, studying each of them in a systematic and logical order.

Take the time to be thorough. As much as possible, find and study every single verse you can that relates to the topic. The only way to know everything God has said about a particular subject is to go through the entire Bible and find all the passages related to that topic. Use your concordance to help you do this.

Finally, be exact. Try to get the exact meaning of every verse you look at in your topical study. Be sure to examine the context of each verse to avoid any possible misinterpretations. The biggest mistake you must avoid is taking a verse out of its context, because doing so could lead to inaccurate conclusions in your topical study.

Example Topical Study: Coats

Study Questions:

1) What are the different types of coats in the Bible?

2) What is the purpose of a coat in the Bible?

Step 1 – Find the Strong's reference number for the word

Coat:
	H3801	*kethoreth*	coat, garment
	H4598	*mehel*	robe, mantel, coat, cloak
	H5622	*serval*	coat
	H8302	*shiryon*	breastplate, coat of mail
	G1903	*ependytes*	fishers coat
	G5509	*chilon*	garment, clothes, coat

Step 2 – Find all the Bible verses using that word

Genesis 37:3	Exodus 28:4	1 Samuel 2:19	Matthew 5:40
Genesis 37:23	Exodus 28:39	1 Samuel 17:5	Luke 6:29
Genesis 37:31	Exodus 29:5	2 Samuel 15:32	John 19:23
Genesis 37:32	Leviticus 8:7	Job 30:18	John 21:7
Genesis 37:33	Leviticus 16:4	Song of Sol. 5:3	

Step 3 – Analyze each verse

Here are some examples of selected verses. When performing your topical studies, you would do this for every Bible verse you found.

Leviticus 8:7 *"girded with a coat"*
Aaron's coat had both practical and symbolic significance.

1 Sam 17:38 *"coat of mail"*
David was about to go fight Goliath, so Saul gave him his armor, which represented Saul's strength and authority. David refused because he had never fought in that armor before, calling it "untried."

John 21:7 *"He girt his fishers coat unto him"*
After His ascension, Jesus appeared to the disciples while they were fishing and told them to cast their nets out again. Peter realized it was Jesus and he put on his coat to seek him.

Step 4 – Sort the verses

Here you would sort the verses into categories. For example, some of the verses refer to regular clothing, while others are talking about ceremonial robes or a suit of armor. So you might divide them into categories such as **Garments**, **Robes**, and **Armor**.

Step 5 – Define your sub-topics

Using the categories you created in step 4, create an outline of your study topic. For example:

    I. Coat as clothing - used for modesty and for protection from the elements
    II. Coat as symbolism - used to represent a higher earthly or spiritual authority
    III. Coat as armor - used for physical protection in battle

Remember this is just an example. Your topical study outline will probably have more points, with sub-points under each main point, depending on how in-depth your chosen topic is. A Bible study on the topic of angels would take much more effort than a study on cows, for instance.

Step 6 – Consult reference materials

Now you can look at what your Bible dictionary, Bible handbook, and Bible encyclopedia have to say on the subject of coats. It's likely you will learn things that you overlooked in your own analysis of the Bible verses, but that's okay. The point of the exercise is for you to build up your own Bible study skills and not be totally reliant on reference materials.

Step 7 – Apply what you've learned

Now you would wrap up your study of coats with a summary paragraph that includes some practical application which you can put to use in your own life.

Exercise 5-1

Tools Needed: *Your Bible, Strong's Concordance, notebook and/or index cards*

Now let's do a topical study together. Actually, you'll be doing all of the work, but I will guide you.

At the end of our word study exercise from chapter 3 (page 26), we determined that the word "care" was the Greek word *merimna* (G3308), which was related to the Greek word *merimnao* (G3309). The English words translated from these two words were: *care, careful,* & *take thought.*

Essentially you have already done step 1 of your topical study when you performed your word study. Now you will pick up from there to perform the rest of the topical study on the word "care."

NOTE: Just reading about this topical study will do you NO GOOD AT ALL! It will only help you if you <u>DO the topical study yourself</u>, and work through the steps on your own. If you aren't willing to set aside the time and effort to do that, just throw this workbook in the trash, because that's what it will be worth to you. You must DO the steps yourself in order to gain any benefit from them.

Complete the following:

A) Look in your Strong's Concordance and make a list of any verses you see for those two words which have a G3308 or a G3309 next to them (step 2)

  1) Write down each verse in your notebook. It's not necessary to write down the entire verse word-for word. As long as you get the gist of the verse, and you're able to distinguish it from the other verses, that's okay.

  2) Instead of writing each verse in your notebook, you might prefer to write each verse down on a separate index card. This will make it easier to move the verses around when you regroup them later.

  3) If the word you've selected for your topical study has a huge number of entries in Strong's Concordance, then you might want to cut & paste them into a text document from your Bible software, or a site like *www.biblegateway.com*.

B) How many verses did you find for G3308 and G3309? _____

Note: Go to the Answer Key on page 65 to check your answers

C) Analyze each verse and add notes to mark commonalities (step 3)

1) Look over the verses in your list and see what common thoughts or ideas emerge.

2) In your notebook or on your index cards, make a note by each verse that shares something in common with another verse.

3) You can use notations or keywords, or even symbols, whatever works for you.

D) Sort the verses so they are matched with similar verses (step 4)

1) If you are using a notebook, you may want to re-write your list of verses on a new page

2) This is where using index cards is helpful, because you can just move the cards around on your desk so they are matched properly

3) If you're using a text document, you can simply cut & paste the verses to move them into your verse groupings.

E) Define your subtopics based on your verse groupings (step 5)

1) Give each group of verses you've sorted a name. These names will become the sub-topics of your topical study outline, which will emerge logically and naturally from your verses.

2) Create an outline based on the sub-topics you've defined.

3) The reason for the outline is to help you communicate to others in an understandable and orderly way that which you have discovered in your topical study.

F) Consult other reference materials (step 6)

1) At this point you can consult outside reference books such as commentaries.

2) You can also get help understanding a difficult verse, if necessary.

3) Hold off on using other reference materials until you have had a chance to thoroughly go over everything yourself, in order to minimize the chance of outside influences mentally blocking revelation from the Holy Spirit.

G) Apply what you've learned (step 7)

1) This is the most important step. This is the reason why you just did all of that work.

2) Find ways to apply your insights into your own life. There will probably be many potential personal applications, so you may need to pick out the most important ones for now.

3) Dig deeper. Your topical study will lead you into new word studies and verse studies. Pray that God will guide you by His Spirit in the direction He wants you to go next.

Exercise 5-2

Tools Needed: *Your Bible, Strong's Concordance, Sword Drills workbook*

Now that you've completed your topical study for the words *merimna* and *merimnao*, I want to share my outline of this same topic. I will also include comments detailing my thought process throughout the outline. This will serve as an example you can look over and review in order to get new ideas for your future topical studies.

Topical Study: Care (G3308 & G3309)

Scripture List & Verse Analysis

Care

Mt 13:22	cares of the world - choke the Word (!)
1 Cor 12:25	care in a good sense, from the church
2 Cor 11:28	negative effects, Paul's worry about the churches
Php 2:20	care in a good sense, from Timothy
1 Pet 5:7	getting free from cares – cast them on the Lord

Careful

Lk 10:41	cares of the world - choke the Word
Php 4:6	getting free from cares – through prayer

Cares

Mk 4:19	cares of the world - choke the Word
Lk 8:14	cares of the world - choke the Word
Lk 21:34	negative effects, could cause me to miss God

Careth

1 Cor 7:32	care in a good sense, believing man caring for things of God
1 Cor 7:33	cares of the world – example: putting wife over God
1 Cor 7:34	care in a good sense, believing man caring for things of God
1 Cor 7:34	cares of the world – example: putting husband over God
1 Pet 5:7	care in a good sense, from God to me

Take Thought

Mt 6:25	cares of the world – example: worrying about my life, food, clothes
Mt 6:31	getting free from cares – take no thought SAYING
Mt 6:34	cares of the world – example: worrying about tomorrow
Mt 10:19	cares of the world – example: worrying about what to say
Lk 12:22	same as Mt 6:25 – important enough to mention twice!

Sorted Subtopic Outline

I. Negative effects of care (worrying)

    A. Cares of the world will CHOKE the seed of God's Word (!)

        1. Listed 4 times: Mt 13:22; Mk 4:19; Lk 8:14; Lk 10:41

        2. This is # 1 danger of worrying. No wonder Satan tempts us to worry!

    B. Cares of the world will cause my thoughts to be pre-occupied with worry

        1. Example: Paul's care for the churches, 2 Cor 11:28

        2. Example: Worrying about my life, food and clothes, Mt 6:25 and Lk 12:22

        (Note: This one was important enough to mention twice!)

        3. Example: Worrying about tomorrow, Mt 6:34

        4. Example: Worrying about what I'm going to say, Mt 10:19

C. Negative effects of cares on my mind, choking God's Word
    1. Could cause me to prioritize my spouse over God, 1 Cor 7:33, 34
    2. Could cause me to miss God in important situations, Lk 21:34

II. How do I get free of the cares of this world?

    A. Cast my cares on the Lord, 1 Pet 5:7
        1. Give all of my worries to Him because He can handle it

    B. How do I cast my cares on Him? Through prayer! Php 4:6

    C. How do I prevent new worries from attaching themselves to me?
        1. Jesus said, "Take no thought (care) SAYING..." Mt 6:31
        2. I need to watch my mouth!

III. Examples of care in a good sense (concern)

    A. The church's concern for other members in the church, 1 Cor 12:25

    B. Timothy praised for his concern for Paul's ministry, Php 2:20

    C. Unmarried man and woman's care for the things of God, 1 Cor 7:32, 34
       (Note: 1 Cor 7:32 starts with the phrase, "But I would have you without carefulness," so I looked up "carefulness" and it is the Greek word "amerimaos" (G275). In Greek the "a-" prefix is a negative, similar to "un-" in English (opened, unopened), so that's why "amerimaos" is translated "without care." Since this is a related word, this is another trail I should explore for this study topic: all Bible verses using G275.)

    D. God's concern for me, 1 Pet 5:7, second word "careth"

Applying What I've Learned

1) I need to recognize the danger of worry

Worrying can be absolutely crippling to my spiritual life. Taking on the cares of this world can even potentially choke the seed of the Word of God from my heart! Worries and cares will attack my thought-life, and could cause me to put other things in front of God, or miss God entirely.

2) I need to repent for worrying

Jesus said we shouldn't worry. That means worrying is a sin, so if I have been allowing myself to be worried then I need to repent. Worry is not something I should dwell on. It's a temptation that needs to be resisted.

3) I need to resist worry

I can get rid of worry that has attached itself to me by praying the prayer of peace, casting my cares on the Lord because He cares for me. I can also resist worry by watching what I say, and making sure that when thoughts or temptation to worry cross my mind, I don't yield to them by giving them voice.

4) There is a good side of caring I need to learn more about

Would this be called caring in a good way? Believers, the church, Timothy, and even God Himself are portrayed in the Bible as caring. The distinction between "good caring" and "bad caring" seems to be caring for the church versus the cares of this world. While it often seems almost effortless to start worrying, exercising that spiritual muscle in the other direction, to care for the things of God and God Himself on purpose, is an area I need to work on and pray about.

Exercise 5-3

Tools Needed: *Your Bible, Strong's Concordance, Sword Drills workbook or your notebook*

Topical studies don't always have to be grand, drawn-out efforts. You may just want to get a quick question answered and a topical study may be your best approach. Consider this example:

There are two different Greek words translated "power" in the New Testament

A) What are these two Greek words? _____ and _____

B) What is the Strong's number for these two Greek words? _____ and _____

C) Briefly define each word:

1.

2.

D) What other English words are used to translate each word?

1.

2.

E) Explain why knowing the difference between these two words could be helpful in your study:

Note: Go to the Answer Key on page 65 to check your answers

Summary

Now that you've seen these examples and worked through the example topical study on your own, you should be ready to launch into your own topical studies.

What Bible topics are the most interesting to you?

Which Bible topics do you want to know more about?

What questions do you have about specific Bible topics?

These questions will lead you into many fruitful and productive topical Bible studies. You might want to start with a smaller topic to begin with, or you may want to begin tackling a large topical study immediately. A larger topic will probably take you several days, or even weeks, but that's fine. You don't have to finish everything in your topical studies in one sitting.

While it's fresh on your mind, use this space to list out some Bible topics that you want to begin studying soon:

Character Studies

I have stored your word up in my heart, that I might not sin against you. – Psalm 119:11

The Character Study method, sometimes called the Biographical Method, studies the life of a certain Bible character. Essentially it's a topical study in which the topic being studied is a person from the Bible. Character studies allow you to evaluate these Bible personalities so you can draw lessons from their lives.

Even though they lived hundreds or even thousands of years ago, people are basically the same. They all have similar needs, wants and desires, which is what makes studying characters in the Bible so beneficial. Paul wrote to the church at Corinth that God gave the stories of the Old Testament to us as examples (Corinthians 10:11). We can actually receive instruction from God as we examine both the good and bad examples shown to us by the characters of the Bible. The steps of a character study are similar to a normal topical study, but with slight variations.

Steps to Perform a Character Study

Step 1 – Find all the Bible verses for that Bible character

Trace out the Bible references for that particular person and, using either paper or index cards, make a list of every Bible verse in which that person is mentioned. It's very likely you'll find references in multiple books. For example, you'll find verses about King David in the writings of Samuel, the Psalms, and the Chronicles. A study of the life of Peter would include verses from all four Gospels.

Step 2 – Analyze each verse

Do this just as you would in a topical study, following the verse study method described in chapter 4. How much time this step takes depends on the number of verses involved. A character study of Moses will take much longer than a character study of Enoch, for example, because there are not as many verses that refer to Enoch. One thing you'll want to look at is the meaning of the name. In the Bible, the meaning of a character's name is always significant and can give you more insights into that character.

Step 3 – Sort the verses

After analyzing each Bible verse, divide the verses into categories, but in this case those categories will usually be phases or events taken from the person's life. For example, a character study of David might divide the verses into David's childhood, when he was a warrior, and when he was King. A character study of Peter might be divided into events such as when Jesus called him to follow, the various Gospel events Peter was involved in, and Peter's career as an Apostle as portrayed in Acts and his two epistles.

Step 4 – Construct a timeline

If you're not quite sure how you should divide the verses into categories, sort the verses chronologically and create a timeline of the Bible character's life. When you do that, patterns will emerge, and the best way to sort the verses will become clearer. Making a timeline will also help you make new connections between the verses, especially if the material for that character is drawn from more than one book in the Bible.

Step 5 – List the Sins and the Wins

Remember that the reason you're getting to know this character is because God has given you information about this person's life so that you can receive instruction and learn from their example. If you're not going to apply the lessons you've learned from the character's life, then why are you even doing this? Take note of the character's attitudes and goals, and record the strengths and weaknesses that are revealed. Look for good examples you can emulate, and be on the lookout for mistakes they made that you can avoid in your own life.

Step 6 – Look for key relationships

The reason people are so interesting to watch is because of the relationships they form with each other, and the same holds true for Bible characters. As you examine the lives of the characters you're studying, look for people in their lives who were influential for any reason, and also look for people whom the Bible character may have influenced. Often these relationships will branch out into exciting new character studies.

Step 7 – Watch out for name variations

Be aware of character name variations and multiple usages of names. For example, Isaiah is called Esaias in the New Testament because that's the Greek spelling of his name. Sometimes the same person goes by multiple names because at some point in the story his name was changed, such as Jacob being renamed Israel, Simon having his name changed to Peter, and Saul being renamed Paul. To get the full picture of these characters, you need to find all the Bible verses for each of the names in question.

Step 8 – Consult reference materials

Finally, after you've gathered all the information from the verses that you can on your own, consult various Bible commentaries to supplement your study efforts. Often you will find the commentators reveal insights and connections you may have missed, but you should still do the initial character study on your own in order to help strengthen your Bible student skillset.

Following Up

Once you've learned all about the Bible character's motives and actions, it will become much easier to get an accurate mental picture of his or her life. As you start getting deeper into Bible character studies, don't be surprised to find yourself getting emotionally attached to these Bible characters, sympathizing with some of their actions, while also intensely disliking some of the choices they make. This is a normal reaction, especially considering that you're going to be able to meet most of them one day

Example Character Study: Jonathan

Step 1 – Find all the Bible verses for that Bible character

Relevant Bible verses:

Judges 18:30	1 Samuel 19:1-7	2 Samuel 1:4-26	2 Samuel 17:17-20
1 Samuel 13:2-23	1 Samuel 20:1-42	2 Samuel 4:4	2 Samuel 21:7-21
1 Samuel 14:1-49	1 Samuel 23:16-18	2 Samuel 9:1-7	1 Chronicles 8:33
1 Samuel 18:1-4	1 Samuel 31:2	2 Samuel 15:27-36	1 Chronicles 9:39

Step 2 – Analyze each verse

Jonathan = "given of God"

Judges 18:30 - different Jonathan, not relevant

1 Samuel 13:2-23 - Jonathan attacked the Philistine garrison at Geba, causing men to flock to Saul to enlist with him in the war against the Philistines. Saul did not wait for the Prophet Samuel to arrive before he offered a sacrifice, which earned a rebuke from Samuel. Jonathan is once again leading soldiers in verse 16, but they don't have enough weapons for the men.

1 Samuel 14:1-49 - Jonathan decides to attack the Philistines without support from his father, Saul. Jonathan and his armor bearer are victorious. He later defies Saul by eating honey after the men were instructed by Saul not to eat. However, Jonathan was not punished by Saul because the people believed God had granted Jonathan the victory.

1 Samuel 18:1-4 - Jonathan and David become close and join in a blood covenant. Jonathan gives David his robe, tunic, sword, bow, and belt.

1 Samuel 19:1-7 - As David becomes more popular, Saul decides to have him killed. Jonathan warns David of Saul's plans, tells him to hide, and tries to reason with Saul. He convinces Saul not to kill David for now.

1 Samuel 20:1-42 - Saul again tries to have David killed, but this time he does not reveal his plans to Jonathan. David and Jonathan renew their covenant, and Jonathan pledges to protect David from Saul. Jonathan warns David that Saul truly means to kill him, and then they part ways.

1 Samuel 23:16-18 - As David is running from Saul, Jonathan encourages him by saying that Saul won't kill him, and one day David will become the King of Israel. They renew their covenant again.

1 Samuel 31:2-6 - In battle with the Philistines on Mount Gilboa, Jonathan and his brothers are killed. Saul convinces his armor bearer to kill him rather than allowing him to be captured alive.

2 Samuel 1:4-26 - David hears of the deaths of Saul and Jonathan. He mourns for them and for Israel. A messenger brings David Saul's crown to David tells him how he killed Saul, hoping to gain David's favor. Instead David has him killed for killing Saul. David leads the people in a lament for the fallen.

2 Samuel 4:4 - Jonathan's son Mephibosheth was lame. When his nurse hears of Jonathan's death, she tries to save his son's life by fleeing Jerusalem.

2 Samuel 9:1-7 - David is now established as the king and wishes to honor his covenant friend Jonathan, so he searches for Jonathan's son. When he finds him, he restores the land that had belonged to his family and promises that he will eat at the king's table from now on.

2 Samuel 15:27-36 - different Jonathan, not relevant

2 Samuel 17:17-20 - different Jonathan, not relevant

2 Samuel 21:7-21 - During David's reign there was a famine, and it was determined the cause of it was Saul's actions against the Gibeonites when he killed their people. David went to them to make things right, and they demanded to know who was left alive from the house of Saul. David gave them everyone that remained, with the exception of Mephibosheth, the son of Jonathan, because of the covenant he had made with Jonathan. The Gibeonites killed all of the remaining members of Saul's family, even including his concubine.

1 Chronicles 8:33 - Genealogy of Saul's family

1 Chronicles 9:39 - Genealogy of Saul's family

Step 3 – Sort the verses

Jonathan, son of Saul
1 Samuel 13:2-23
1 Samuel 14:1-44, 49

Jonathan's Death
1 Samuel 31:2
2 Samuel 1:4-26

Jonathan, friend of David
1 Samuel 18:1-4
1 Samuel 19:1-7
1 Samuel 20:1-42
1 Samuel 23:16-18

Jonathan's Legacy
2 Samuel 4:4
2 Samuel 9:1-7
2 Samuel 21:7-21
1 Chronicles 8:33
1 Chronicles 9:39

Step 4 – Construct a timeline

1) Jonathan was raised in Saul's house and was a leader in his army. He was the presumptive heir to the throne.

2) Jonathan met David when David slew Goliath and began ministering to his father, Saul. Their friendship grew, and they made a covenant with each other.

3) As David's influence grew, Jonathan realized that David was the one God had anointed to be the King. While he continued to serve his father Saul, Jonathan remained loyal to David and protected him to honor their covenant.

4) While at war with the Philistines, Jonathan and Saul were both killed in battle.

5) David mourned his friend Jonathan, and honored their covenant by protecting and providing for his son Mephibosheth.

Step 5 – List the Sins and the Wins

Sins:
- Disobeyed Saul when he ate honey after Saul had commanded that none should eat
- Disobeyed Saul to warn David (whether this was a "sin" or not is debatable!)

Wins:
- Excellent character
- Good leader, athletic
- Loyal friend: he worked hard to balance the interests of both David and Saul
- Mighty warrior: almost single-handedly slew the Philistine garrison at Geba

Step 6 – Look for key relationships

Jonathan & Saul

Jonathan was loyal to Saul as both a father, military leader, and king until he recognized that Saul had lost the anointing to be king. While he became loyal to David as God's anointed, he still served Saul in the war against the Philistines, even up to his death.

Jonathan and David

Jonathan formed his relationship with David independent of his father, and he eventually solidified their bond with a blood covenant. This powerful agreement extended even beyond the death of Jonathan, and David honored it when he took in Jonathan's son.

David and Saul

While their relationship began encouragingly, it became hostile as Saul's downward spiral continued. Even though Saul repeatedly threatened David, David never returned the animosity and even went out of his way to honor Saul when he could, including killing the messenger who claimed he had killed Saul. As it relates to Jonathan, David's behavior and decisions no doubt made it easier for Jonathan, who was caught between the two rivals.

Jonathan and the People

The people loved Jonathan. When he disobeyed Saul and ate the wild honey, they rose up in his defense, noting that God still blessed Jonathan even while he was disobedient toward Saul. Jonathan could have easily tried to leverage this popular support to help him gain the throne that, according to tradition, would be rightfully his when Saul died. However, the high quality of Jonathan's character prevented him from attempting to take advantage of that.

Step 7 – Watch out for name variations

There are no other name variations for Jonathan in the Old or New Testament.

Step 8 – Consult reference materials

Author and Bible scholar Reverend Thomas Hunter Weir describes Jonathan's life in three distinct periods: 1) as Saul's heir, 2) as a friend of David, and 3) Saul's persecution of David during David's exile.

Exercise 6-1

Tools Needed: *Your Bible, Strong's Concordance, Sword Drills workbook or notebook*

Character study of Abel

The character of Abel is introduced in the Bible in Genesis 4. Using your concordance, look up all of the references to Abel in the New Testament.

In the space below, list some things you learned about Abel that you didn't know before:

Note: Go to the Answer Key on page 65 to check your answers

Exercise 6-2

Tools Needed: *Your Bible, Strong's Concordance, Sword Drills workbook or notebook*

Character study of Enoch

The character of Enoch is introduced in the Bible in Genesis 5. Using your concordance, look up all of the references to Enoch in the New Testament.

What are some things you learned about him that you didn't know before?

Note: Go to the Answer Key on page 65 to check your answers

The character studies chosen for these exercises were deliberately chosen because they are limited in scope. The limited number of references allowed for a quick illustration on how to perform a character study. Character studies are usually much more extensive.

For example, a character study on Abraham, Moses, David, or Paul would take more effort, due to the greater number of Bible references for those two individuals. A character study of Jeremiah or Ezekiel would include a study of the books written under their name, in addition to references to them in other parts of the Bible.

When you've done studies on two related characters, such as David and King Saul, then you will gain deeper insights into how they interacted with each other as well. You will begin to feel like you know these people personally, and the more in-depth your character studies are, the more fascinating those characters will become.

Chapter 7
Chronological Studies

Open my eyes, that I may behold wondrous things out of your law. - Psalm 119:11

A chronological Bible study combines the topical study and the character study methods, studying the lives of Bible characters or Bible events in their historical order. This is also very helpful for putting Bible passages in their proper context, and can be easily done using the tools described in the previous chapter.

An example of an interesting chronological Bible study could be listing out the events in the life of David, and then inserting individual Psalms into the chronology at the times when they were written. This would allow you to see what was happening in David's life when he wrote each Psalm, and would also give you greater understanding into the Psalm itself.

Steps to Perform a Chronological Study

Step 1 – Decide what event you want to study

This can be almost anything you want it to be. Maybe you have some questions about how a particular set of circumstances came into being at the start of a Bible story. Perhaps you are curious about what causes led to certain effects. Chronological studies are great for breaking down a complex series of events.

Step 2 – Determine the main Scripture passage for that event

What is the main Scripture passage where this Bible event is covered? Where in the Bible is the most material about your event found? This is where you will want to begin.

Step 3 – Find other Scripture passages that also touch on that event

What other passages in the Bible touch on that same event? These are other locations where material concerning the event you are studying can be found.

Step 4 – Create a timeline of the pieces that make up the event

Using your main Scripture passage as the foundation, insert pieces from the other related passages where they best fit. This could be more detailed information about what's already in the main passage, or new information that the first passage doesn't contain. When you've blended all the pieces together in their correct order, then you will have a complete picture of that Bible event.

Step 5 – What Bible characters are associated with the event?

Look at the characters that are involved with this Bible event. What was each character's point of view about what happened? What motivated each character in the story to do what they did? What were their goals, or what was each character trying to achieve? What key choices were made by any of the characters that affected the course of events in the story?

Step 6 – Examine the What If's

Now think about what could have happened differently in the story. What should have happened vs. what actually did happen? What if certain characters had made different choices? In what ways might better choices have caused a different outcome? This is very useful because it allows you to learn from the mistakes made by characters in the Bible, instead of having to learn them on your own.

Step 7 – Identify the life lessons you can apply

This is the most important step. It's not enough just to be proud of yourself for figuring out all of the intricacies of a particular Bible event. You have to be able to pull lessons out of it which you can then apply to your own life. Can you relate to what any of the characters thought, said or did? What can you learn from their example? What mistakes did they make that you could avoid? What did they do right that you could emulate in your life?

Following Up

The chronological study method combines many of the study methods you've learned up to this point, and it can be one of the most effective ways to really get a feel for how a series of Bible events flowed together. You won't always need to go to the lengths of a full chronological study to find the answers to your Bible questions, but you will find that this type of Bible study will almost always branch off into other exciting studies, and this will allow you to build up your understanding of the Bible more and more.

Exercise 7-1: Example Chronological Study

Tools Needed: *Your Bible, Gospel Harmony (optional), Sword Drills workbook or notebook*

In the Gospel of Matthew we read of the preaching of John the Baptist and the baptism of Jesus, followed by His anointing by the Holy Spirit and then the 40 days of temptation by Satan in the wilderness (Matthew 3:11 - 4:11). This episode is also included in the other synoptic Gospels (Mark 1:7-13 and Luke 3:15 - 4:13).

(Note: The prefix syn means "same," and optic means "look," so synoptic means "looks the same." The books of Matthew, Mark, and Luke are often called the synoptic gospels because they are very similar.)

In John's Gospel we also read about the opening days of Jesus' ministry (John 1:19-28). A seven-day sequence is given, ending with Jesus' first miracle at the wedding of Cana (John 2:1-11). From that point forward, Jesus begins His ministry in Galilee of preaching, teaching and healing.

Now here's the big question:

In the Gospel of John, what happened to the 40 days of temptation of Jesus in the wilderness?

Where can we possibly fit that event into these seven days as John describes them? Obviously we can't, so how can we possibly reconcile John's account of the beginning of Jesus' ministry with the version that's portrayed in the synoptic gospels?

Isn't this exactly the sort of question that gives critics of the Bible ammunition to make their case that the Word of God is full of alleged contradictions?

Using a chronological Bible study, let's try to figure this out.

Step 1 – Decide what event you want to study

We are studying the water baptism of Jesus in the Jordan River, and the timing of that event in relation to the events of John 1:19-2:11. We know that Scripture cannot contradict other Scripture, so our task is to reconcile the opening events of Jesus' ministry in John's gospel with the opening events of Jesus' ministry in the synoptic gospels.

Step 2 – Determine the main Scripture passage for that event

The main passage is John 1:19-2:11.

Step 3 – Find other Scripture passages that also touch on that event

Related Scripture passages are Matthew 3:11-4:11; Mark 1:7-13; and Luke 3:15 –4:13.

Step 4 – Create a timeline of the pieces that make up the event

Day 1 - John 1:19-28 - The ministry and message of John the Baptist, the Pharisees question him

Day 2 - John 1:29-34 - The "next day" (v.29) Jesus arrives and we learn about His baptism and anointing

Day 3 - John 1:35-42 - "Again the next day" (v.35) Jesus calls the first two of the Twelve Disciples to follow Him: Andrew and John (the author of John's gospel, not John the Baptist). Andrew and John had been disciples of John the Baptist, but when they heard him testifying about Jesus the day before, they left John the Baptist to follow Jesus instead.

Day 4 - John 1:43-51 - "The day following" (v.43) Jesus calls the next two of the Twelve, Philip and Nathaniel.

Day 5 and **Day 6** - no information given

Day 7 - John 2:1-11 - The "third day" after that, Jesus attends the wedding at Cana.

Step 5 – What Bible characters are associated with the event?

John the Baptist, the Pharisees, Jesus, John the disciple, Andrew, Philip, and Nathaniel.

Step 6 – Examine the What If's

In this case, we still need to look at all of the gospel accounts and reconcile them. What do you think the solution to this puzzle might be?

Note: Go to the Answer Key on page 65 to check your answers

Step 7 – Identify the life lessons you can apply

Aside from the many insights you can gain from watching the various characters interact in this episode, you can also reaffirm your confidence in the fact that the Bible is truly inspired by the Holy Spirit, and even when there are apparent conflicts in the Scripture, there is always a way to reconcile them.

Exercise 7-2

Tools Needed: *Your Bible, Strong's Concordance, Sword Drills workbook or notebook*

Most people have read the story of David and Goliath in 1 Samuel 17. Stop here and go read 1 Samuel 17 now if you need to refresh yourself on the details. Then read 1 Samuel 21:1-10.

A) Whose sword does David take with him when he leaves? _____

B) What city did the original owner of the sword come from? _____

C) What do you think the people of that city thought when David showed up there carrying that particular sword?

_____

Now read 1 Samuel 21:10-15.

D) What are your impressions of this event in David's life? What do you make of David's odd behavior in this passage?

_____

E) How does knowing some of the background (from the Scriptures above) enhance your reading of this passage?

_____

Now read Psalm 56.

F) What are your impressions of this Psalm?

_____

Note the heading above Psalm 56:1 (if your Bible has that), which notes that David wrote this Psalm during this specific event in his life.

G) How does Psalm 56 help you to better understand the story in 1 Samuel 21:10-15?

_____

H) How does knowing the events of 1 Samuel 21:10-15 enhance your reading of Psalm 56?

_____

I) What new insights do you gain from Psalm 56 by placing it in its chronological setting?

_____

Note: Go to the Answer Key on page 65 to check your answers

Chapter 8

Book Background Studies

And these words which I command you today shall be in your heart. You shall teach them diligently to your children, and shall talk of them when you sit in your house, when you walk by the way, when you lie down, and when you rise up. - Deuteronomy 6:6, 7

The goal of the book survey study is to gain a better understanding of the background of a particular book of the Bible before you study the book itself, so that your study of that book will be more effective.

Steps to Perform a Book Background Study

Step 1 – Choose a book of the Bible to study

For beginners it's a good idea to pick a shorter book, but it should also be a book you have a greater interest in, because that will help to motivate you through the study.

Step 2 – Assemble your reference tools

You should have a Bible handbook, a Bible Atlas, Bible commentaries for that book, and a Bible dictionary or Bible encyclopedia. Bible students will usually prefer some reference tools over others, so keep track of which reference tools you use and make a note of the ones that are the most helpful so you can return to them in future studies.

Step 3 – Attempt to discover the following:

- Who is the author of the book?
- Where was the author when the book was written?
- What was the geographical setting of the book?
- Who was the original intended audience of the book?
- What is the date of the book?
- What historical events occurred just prior to the time the book was being written?
- What historical events occurred during the time the book was written?
- What historical events occurred immediately after the book was written?
- What future events or persons are anticipated in the book?
- What was the reigning culture of the day?
- What was the current political situation?
- Why do you think the author wrote the book?
- How does the book fit into the overall arc of the Bible story?

Step 4 – Summarize your research

At this point you should have a rough idea what the book is about. Organize your notes on index cards or in an outline in a way that's most useful to you.

Step 5 – Create a personal goal for further study

Write down your personal goal for further study of that book. At this point it's likely you've come across something about the book that's piqued your curiosity enough to interest you to find out more. It might be one of the themes covered in the book, or maybe it's a certain Bible character, or any number of possibilities. As you study this Bible book more using the Bible study methods in the chapters that follow, you'll learn many different things along the way, but make a note of one specific thing you're going to be focusing on.

Exercise 8-1

Tools Needed: *Bible Surveys, Bible Commentaries, Bible Handbook and Bible Encyclopedia*

Step 1 – Choose a book of the Bible to study

For this exercise, let's do a book survey study of Paul's second letter to Timothy.

Step 2 – Assemble your reference tools

Consult the Bible study resources listed above along with any others you might have (including online resources if available).

Step 3 – Attempt to discover the following:

A) Who is the author of the book? _____

B) Where was the author when the book was written? _____

C) What was the geographical setting of the book? _____

D) Who was the original intended audience of the book? _____

E) What is the date of the book? _____

F) What historical events occurred just prior to the time the book was being written?

_____

G) What historical events occurred during the time the book was written?

_____

H) What historical events occurred immediately after the book was written?

_____

I) What future events or persons are anticipated in the book?

_____

J) What was the reigning culture of the day? _____

K) What was the current political situation? _____

L) Why do you think the author wrote the book?

_____

M) How does the book fit into the overall arc of the Bible story?

_____

Note: Go to the Answer Key on page 65 to check your answers

Step 4 – Summarize your research

As you were doing your research on the background of 2 Timothy in order to answer the questions in Step 3, you probably came across some things that interested you, such as new facts or key Bible verses. In the space below, write out a short summary of what you picked up on in your book background study of 2 Timothy:

Step 5 – Create a personal goal for further study

From what you wrote down in Step 4, you probably have some new ideas or found new directions for future Bible studies. This could be a character study on Paul or Timothy, a verse study or a word study, or a topical study of one of the subjects mentioned in the epistle.

Pick the one that's most interesting to you, or the one that you think would be the most helpful to you, and make a note of it below, so you can pursue that goal in your future Bible study sessions.

Chapter 9
Book Survey Studies

The Jews proved more generous-minded than those in Thessalonica, for they accepted the message most eagerly and studied the Scriptures every day to see if what they were now being told were true. - Acts 17:11 (PHL)

The purpose of the book survey study is to obtain a detailed overview of a particular book of the Bible. When used together with the study methods described in the next two chapters (the Chapter Study and the Book Synthesis Study), it will give the Bible student a comprehensive view of each book of the Bible.

The main goal of the book survey method is to gain a detailed understanding as to why the book was written, its context, its theme, its structure, and its content.

Steps to Perform a Book Survey Study

Step 1 – Read the book following these steps:

Read the whole book through in one sitting

The two longest books of the Bible are Psalms and Isaiah, and the average reader can get through those in just a few hours. Reading the book straight through in one sitting gives you a good overview of its contents. The larger books can be divided into two sections if necessary, so you can read them with a break in between, but you should still read it all the way through as fast as possible.

Read the book in a modern translation

You will want to read the book in a translation where the language is current so it won't distract you from the content of the book.

Read the book as though the chapter and verse divisions weren't there

Read the book like you would any regular book, ignoring the chapter and verse reference numbers. This will give you a better feel for the flow of the book and how the various ideas in the book relate to one another.

Read through the book three times

You will be surprised at what you notice in your second and third readings that you missed the first time through.

Read without referring to external notes

Concentrate on the text of the book itself without using any commentaries or study notes at this point.

Read through the book prayerfully

Ask God to speak to you by His Holy Spirit as you read, and pray that He opens your eyes to the lessons He wants you to learn.

Step 2 – Make notes on what you read

Take detailed notes as you read, and write down your observations about what you're reading, especially during the second and third times through. Write down your impressions of the book and any important details that you uncover. Use these questions to help you:

What genre is the book?

Is the book law, historic, poetic, prophetic, biographic, correspondence, or narrative?

What do you think was the author's purpose?

Make note of your first impressions as you read.

What words does the author use most often?

What words does the author seem to consider to be important or significant?

Is there a key verse or a key statement?

For example, is there a verse like Revelation 1:19 which summarizes the entire Book of Revelation?

What is the literary style of the author?

How does the writing style relate to the book's message?

Does the author reveal his emotions in the writing?

How would the original readers have responded to this emotion? How do you respond to this emotion?

What do you believe the main theme is?

Make note of the main theme (or themes) of the book. Does the book have a major thrust or overall idea?

How is the book organized?

What are the organic divisions of the book? What influenced those natural divisions in the book (people, geography, historical events, culture)? Remember that the chapters and verses (and in some translations, even paragraphs) were all added centuries after the original authors completed their work, so don't let those influence your answer to this question. Instead, look for divisions that emerge naturally from the book.

What people are central to the book?

Are there specific characters that are important? If so what part do they play in this book?

Step 3 – Do a background study of the book

If you have already done a Book Background study of that Bible book (as described in chapter 8), that will already contain useful information you can refer to for this study. If not, go ahead and do a Book Background study of the book now.

Step 4 – Make a horizontal chart of the book's contents

A horizontal chart is a visual representation of the book on one or more sheets of paper. It allows you to grasp the general details of the book as you draw them out pictorially. Follow these steps to create your horizontal chart:

Draw out the chapters

On a single sheet of paper, or more if needed, make as many vertical columns as there are chapters in the book you are studying.

Read through the book a fourth time

As you read through the book again you should start noticing some major divisions. These will often match the chapter divisions, but not always. Write out headings for each of your major divisions using as few words as possible.

Read through the book a fifth time

As you do this, think of a short title for each chapter and write them down just below the divisions you made in the previous step, placing each at the top of your columns. Good chapter titles are short, usually just one to four words. They should be picturesque descriptions, helping you to visualize the chapter contents, but they should also be taken from the text if possible. Each chapter title should be unique, and not repeated from chapter titles in other book studies.

Read through the book a sixth time

This time through the book you will create a series of titles for the paragraphs within each chapter. If you're reading a version that uses only Bible verses without paragraphs, divide the chapter into paragraph divisions that seem most logical to you. Most every modern translation will already be divided into paragraphs, however.

NOTE: a sample horizontal chapter outline chart can be found on the next page.
You may photocopy that page, or download a blank horizontal book outline chart at :
http://biblestudy.michaeldorseyonline.com

Step 5 - Create a basic outline of the book

Drawing from all the work you've done so far, create a preliminary outline of the book. You will use this again later in chapter 11 when you learn about the Book Synthesis Study in which you will make a more detailed outline of the book. Here are some helpful points:

Start your outline

List the major points of the book and organize them into an outline.

Organize your outline

Put the major points of your outline in sequence of descending importance. List the major points first followed by the minor points.

Refer to your notes

The chapter and paragraph titles you created will be helpful with your outline since they are usually grouped around the major ideas.

Bible Chapter Analysis Chart

Book/Chapter:	Book/Chapter:	Book/Chapter:	Book/Chapter:
Chapter Title:	Chapter Title:	Chapter Title:	Chapter Title:
Characters:	Characters:	Characters:	Characters:
Events:	Events:	Events:	Events:
Key Verses:	Key Verses:	Key Verses:	Key Verses:
Major Themes:	Major Themes:	Major Themes:	Major Themes:

Step 6 – Create a goal for personal study

This is the same as Step 5 in the book background study. During your study, some things probably jumped out at you that you want to look at further. At this point you may have already reached the goal you set in your book background study, or you may be closer to it than you were. If you have met your personal goal, then create a new one based on the work you've put in so far. If you're still working toward the goal you set in the previous study, you might want to make some adjustments based on some of the new things you've learned.

Exercise 9-1

Tools Needed: *Your Bible, Strong's Concordance, horizontal chapter chart or notebook*

Now that we are getting into the more advanced types of Bible studies, it's harder to walk you through every part of it step by step. By now you should have enough knowledge about Bible study methods to perform these things on your own. At this point, it really comes down to this:

Will you put in the effort and do the work necessary to dig into God's Word for yourself?

The book survey study requires reading through a single book of the Bible several times. I can't put that in an example for you. You will have to do that on your own. If you are really hungry for God's Word, and you really want to discipline yourself to learn how to study it out, then this won't be a problem for you.

So let's get started! Pick a book of the Bible to survey, any book you want. I suggest you select a shorter book to get started, one that's no longer than 6 chapters.

Following the Steps

Depending on the length of the book you've selected, a Book Survey study could take you several hours or even several days. Most likely you will need to plan out a schedule for your study, but you don't want it to stretch out for too long. After all, it is a survey, not an in-depth study.

Remember, the Book Survey study is only the surface level of a comprehensive 3-part book study, so when you're ready to really go deeper into the book you've chosen, you can continue to chapters 10 and 11.

NOTE: a sample horizontal book outline chart can be found on the next page.

You may photocopy that page, or download a blank horizontal book outline chart at :

http://biblestudy.michaeldorseyonline.com

Book Analysis Chart

Book Title: Author: Genre: Setting: Original Audience:	**Key words and phrases**

First Impressions

What was the author's purpose for writing the book?

How would the original intended audience have received the message?

What seems to be the main theme of the book?

How is the book organized or laid out?

Major Characters	**Questions List** (things I want to learn more about)

Chapter 10
Chapter Analysis Studies

For the word of God is quick, and powerful, and sharper than any two-edged sword, piercing even to the dividing asunder of soul and spirit, and of the joints and marrow, and is a discerner of the thoughts and intents of the heart. - Hebrews 4:12 (KJV)

Expository Bible study is the opposite of a topical Bible study, which gathers verses on a single topic from all over the Bible. Instead, the expository Bible study method focuses on just a single passage of text. Usually this is a single Bible chapter, thus the name chapter analysis study, but it could also be a complete story that is only a part of a Bible chapter. This is also sometimes referred to as inductive Bible study.

You may have heard the term "expository sermon," in which a minister preaches from a single passage of text, rather than jumping all over the Bible preaching about a certain topic (which is called a topical sermon). The objective of an expository sermon, and of expository Bible study, is to "expose" what the text is actually saying to us.

The Chapter Analysis Study picks up where the Book Survey Study ends. Now that you have a good grasp of the overall picture of the book, what it means, why it was written, and so forth, you can begin to examine the individual parts that make up the book. The easiest way to subdivide a book of the Bible is to use the already existing chapter divisions so you can study each chapter in detail.

The Chapter Analysis Study is the second of three methods of Bible study that will give you a very in-depth view of a particular book of the Bible. These three methods take a lot of work, but they also produce the greatest results. You will need your usual kit of Bible reference tools on hand for this study, including several Bible translations, Bible dictionaries, handbooks, encyclopedias, Bible commentaries, and Old and New Testament surveys.

Steps to Perform a Chapter Analysis Study

Step 1 – Create a chapter summary

First read the chapter several times through. If you're studying a certain Bible book, this will usually be the first chapter of that book. However, you could also analyze a favorite chapter such as Psalm 91 or John 15, or even a portion of a chapter, such as the "armor of God" section of Ephesians 6. After you have read the chapter through several times, describe the content of the chapter, and find a way of summarizing it using one of the following methods:

Outline the chapter

Create an outline of the chapter based on the internal paragraph divisions in the chapter. Give each paragraph a heading and put any sub-points within the paragraph underneath it. This is similar to the outline you made in the Book Survey study last chapter, but this time it's only for the single chapter.

Rewrite the chapter

When you rewrite it, leave out any modifying clauses or phrases. Use only the subjects, verbs, and objects. This can be challenging, but the result is a vastly simplified record of what happened in the chapter.

Paraphrase the chapter

Rephrase the chapter in your own words. This should be done in a way that would allow another person to clearly understand it.

Step 2 – Observation: What does this passage say?

The next step in exposing the text is to simply observe it for yourself. Try to let go of any presuppositions you might have about the passage in question. Don't try to force the text into your own teaching outline. Instead, let the outline of the passage emerge naturally from the text as you observe it. To help you observe the passage, ask the standard questions a news reporter would ask: Who is involved? What happened? What was taught? When? Where? How? Why? This will allow you to discover what the author is trying to say.

Record your observations and insights. Look at every detail of the chapter, examining each sentence and word, and writing down everything you see. Look for key words or repeated words or phrases in the passage. See if you can find any warnings or commands. Here is a list of things you should look for:

- Key words
- Repeated words and phrases
- Questions being asked
- Answers being given
- Commands
- Warnings
- Comparisons - things that are alike
- Contrasts - things that are different
- Illustrations
- Causes and effects for why things happen
- Motivations causing characters to take certain actions
- Promises and their conditions for fulfillment
- Progression from the general to the specific or from the specific to the general
- Steps of progression in a narrative or biography
- Lists of things
- Advice or admonitions
- The tone of the passage - attitudes and emotional atmosphere
- Explanations
- Old Testament quotes in the New Testament
- References to current events in the time it was written

Pray to God and ask for the Holy Spirit's guidance. Slowly read the passage over and over again, turning it over in your mind. Look at the passage in different Bible versions and see what else you notice.

Step 3 – Interpretation: What does this passage mean?

Ask detailed questions of the chapter. What is the author's intent in this passage? What is the major principle or lesson which the writer (and the Holy Spirit who inspired him) wanted to communicate? How was his message relevant to his audience, the people of that day? How would they have understood what he was saying?

Take note of each question you ask, even if you aren't able to find the answer right away. The time may come when you find the answer during another study and then you'll be able to place it here as well.

Observe the context of the passage

If you've already done a Book Survey Study for this book, that will be helpful to you here.

Define the words and phrases used

Make use of your Bible reference tools to insure that you have the correct understanding of the key words and phrases within the passage. Use a Bible dictionary to define any unfamiliar words or ideas.

Look at the structure and grammar of the passage

This can help you to understand the flow of ideas and concepts within the passage, enabling you to see how they stand in relation to each other.

Use other Bible translations

Look at other translations to see whether they are more understandable. Often another translation will have slightly different wording that will shine a little more light on the passage.

View the passage against its background

As needed, use Bible study helps to get a clearer meaning of the passage, such as Bible dictionaries and encyclopedias, or a Bible study guide for the text, subject, or person that is being studied.

Refer to a commentary as a last resort

If all other means have failed, you can always refer to a Bible commentary to compare your interpretation of the passage with that of the commentator. The reason this should be the last resort is because if you look at the commentary first, it will bias your own interpretations as you discover them.

Once again, pray for the Holy Spirit's guidance as you think these questions through and try to determine the main idea or principle lesson of the passage. Why do you think God put this in the Bible?

Step 4 – Compare your chapter with other Bible passages

Now look at other Scriptures that relate to this passage. See what other passages in the Bible say about the concepts covered in this chapter. These can usually be found in the center marginal notes of Bibles or in footnotes. What do these other related verses reveal to you about the author's thoughts or ideas?

Step 5 – Make a list of potential life applications from the passage

Now look at your own life. What is the Holy Spirit saying to YOU in this passage? Ask Him and wait quietly for a moment to see what thoughts and impressions you get. Make sure you take note of anything that comes to you so it doesn't slip away later.

Next, think about your life in relation to the passage you've just studied. Ask yourself "What is one practical way I can apply the main idea of this passage to my life?" Usually more than one application idea will come to you. Be sure you take them all down.

This is a list you are making for future reference. You don't want to try to apply everything that you write here, but in step seven (below) you will choose one of these applications to start working into your daily life.

Step 6 – Draw your own conclusions

Review the first five steps of this study, then come up with some initial conclusions about the chapter and write them down. As you do this, you might discover additional connections within the chapter, which will lead to new ideas about the chapter. Take note of those as well.

Step 7 – Application – How can I apply this principle to my life?

Write down one life application from the list you made in step five. Be sure that it is both practical and applicable to your life personally. Remember to return to your written application in the near future so you can evaluate your progress.

Finally, consider your attitude and your actions. What will you do differently based on what you've learned? It doesn't have to be some huge mountain-moving thing. Most of the time spiritual growth is very gradual and hardly noticeable when it's happening. Only later when you look back and realize how far you've come will you recognize how God was helping you along the whole time.

Exercise 10-1

Tools Needed: *Your Bible, Sword Drills workbook or notebook*

Read chapter 1 of 1 John. What are the natural divisions of this chapter? Give each section of the chapter a title and write them out in the space below:

Note: Go to the Answer Key on page 65 to check your answers

Summary

These are the steps for a Chapter Analysis Study that will allow you to expose all of the treasures that are buried within the text of a Bible passage. Topical studies can be useful and definitely have their place, but nothing is as profitable as dealing directly with a specific text from God's Word.

Another advantage of expository studies is you don't have to be "feeling it" first in order to get into a good session of Bible study. The text is the text, and you can look at it and analyze it whether you're feeling spiritual at the moment or not. When you do this, you'll find that what will usually happen is the discipline of studying will actually motivate you into a more spiritual mood.

Finally, while an expository study can be focused on a shorter passage or story contained within a chapter, this is also the best study method to use for chapter studies. When you can break down an entire Bible chapter using the expository study method, you'll see links between the stories within the chapter that you may have missed before. There's a reason the author put his book in that particular order, and when you start to make those connections, new revelation and insight that you've never seen before will be opened up to you.

Chapter 11

Book Synthesis Studies

*Don't let the world around you squeeze you into its own mold, but let
God re-mold your minds from within, so that you may prove in practice
that the plan of God for you is good, meets all his demands and moves
towards the goal of true maturity. - Romans 12:2 (PHL)*

The word "synthesis" means the combining of the separate elements of material into a single or unified whole. The Book Synthesis study, you will summarize and compact the results of your Book Survey study and your Chapter Analysis studies, putting the details you pulled from the book back together again.

These three methods, taken together, require a high level of effort on your part, but they will ultimately yield the most thorough results in your study of any book of the Bible. You will use the same Bible reference tools you used in the previous two Bible study methods, along with your Book Survey and Chapter Analysis studies that you created. You will need to refer to them often during your Book Synthesis study.

Steps to Perform a Book Synthesis Study

Step 1 – Reread the book several times

Do this in the same manner as you did in the Book Survey study (as described in chapter 9), taking notes as you go.

Step 2 – Write out a detailed final outline

Start with the preliminary outline from your Book Survey study, and the summaries from your Chapter Analysis studies. Combine these with the notes from your readings in step 1 to write out your outline in its final form.

Step 3 – Write a descriptive book title

To do this, use the same methods you followed to give titles to each part of your Chapter Analysis study (as described in chapter 10). Try to make the title original, defining the contents of the book in as few words as possible.

Step 4 – Make a summary of your insights

Based on what you discovered in your previous Book Survey study and Chapter Analysis studies of this book of the Bible, summarize your conclusions on the major and minor ideas of the book. Don't look at any published Bible commentaries yet, since the goal is to arrive at your own understanding of this book of the Bible. You can also include any new ideas you discovered during your readings from step one.

Step 5 – Write out a personal application

Go back through the Book Survey study and your Chapter Analysis studies which you did for this Bible book, and review all the personal goals and applications that your study generated. Take note of any that are still not completed, and create a plan to reach those remaining goals as soon as possible. If you were able to complete all of your personal goals and applications, look for new ones, and make a plan to implement those in your life as well.

Step 6 – Share the results of your study

As you became a more proficient Bible student, you will eventually find yourself teaching or leading Bible studies. If you've come this far and successfully stuck with it, by now you should have a solid chunk of material gathered on the Bible book that you've been studying.

Now it's time to share the fruit of your efforts with others who share your interest in the Word of God. You may not be called to the ministry of the teacher, or to the Teacher's office (Ephesians 4:11), but that doesn't mean you can't share your new insights with your brothers and sisters of like precious faith.

As a part of the Body of Christ (Ephesians 4:13-16; 1 Corinthians 12:12-27), you are called to minister to your fellow believers. Remember that although we are saved individually through Jesus Christ, our faith is lived out within a community. Pray to God that He will give you guidance as to when would be an appropriate time to share the things He's revealed to you.

Now what?

If you've done a comprehensive study of your chosen Bible book using all three of these study methods (the Book Survey study, the Chapter Analysis study, and the Book Synthesis study), then at this point you probably have a better understanding of that book than 99% of the Christians who are alive on the Earth today.

Take a moment and let that sink in. How grateful are you to be able to study the Word of God in such an in-depth and thorough manner?

Now all that's left for you to do is decide where do you want to go from here? You may want to select another book from the Bible and restart the entire process.

Perhaps something in the book you've just finished studying caught your attention, and now you want to start a topical study in order to obtain a deeper understanding of that particular Bible subject.

Maybe since you've gained a greater understanding of the Bible book you've just finished, you want to see how it ties in to other Bible books, so a chronological study may be in order.

It's also possible that the you came across one or more interesting Bible characters during your study of this book of the Bible, and you want to do a character study to learn more about them, and why they made the choices they made.

The bottom line is you can go wherever the Spirit of God and your desires lead you. You will never plumb the depths of the Bible in this lifetime, but adventures in Bible discovery await you, and now you have the tools and training you need to take advantage of them.

Answer Key

Here are the answers to the exercises found in Sword Drills. They are numbered in order by chapter, with the page number in parenthesis to help you locate them more easily.

Exercise 2-2 (page 20)

A) Genesis, Exodus, Leviticus, Numbers, Deuteronomy
   - from the Pentateuch section of the Old Testament

B) Job, Psalms, Proverbs, Ecclesiastes, Song of Solomon
   - from the Poetry Books section of the Old Testament

C) Isaiah, Jeremiah, Lamentations, Ezekiel, Daniel
   - from the Major Prophets section of the Old Testament

D) Matthew, Mark, Luke, John, Acts
   - from the Gospels and History sections of the New Testament

E) Romans, Galatians, Ephesians, Philippians, Colossians
   - from the Pauline Epistles section of the New Testament

F) James, 2 Peter, 1 John, 3 John, Jude
   - from the General Epistles section of the New Testament

G) Pentateuch, Historical Books, Poetry Books, Major Prophets, Minor Prophets
   - from the Old Testament

H) Gospels, History, Pauline Epistles, General Epistles, Prophecy
   - from the New Testament

I) Fill in the blanks: 1) Judges   2) I Kings   3) Esther   4) Obadiah

J) Hosea - Joel - Amos - Obadiah - Jonah - Micah - Nahum - Habakkuk - Zephaniah - Haggai - Zechariah - Malachi

K) Fill in the blanks: 1) 2 Timothy   2) John   3) 1 Peter   4) Ephesians

L) Romans - 1 Corinthians - 2 Corinthians - Galatians - Ephesians - Philippians - Colossians - 1 Thessalonians - 2 Thessalonians - 1 Timothy - 2 Timothy - Titus - Philemon

M) Fill in the blanks: 1) B   2) A   3) D   4) C

Exercise 3-1 (page 24)

A) Find the verse:

   1) 2 Corinthians 9:7

   2) Psalm 105:15; 1 Chronicles 16:22

   3) n/a - there is no such verse in the Bible

Exercise 3-1 (page 24) - continued

B) Four Parts of a Concordance:

1) Main Concordance

2) Appendix

3) Dictionary of Hebrew Words

4) Dictionary of Greek Words

C) Word Study on Praise:

1) 7 words for praise

2) Halal, Yadah, Towdah, Shabach, Barak, Zamar, and Tehillah

3) Halal - to be clear, to boast, to show, rave, celebrate, be clamorously foolish

Yadah - the extended hand, to throw out the hand; opposite of hand-wringing

Towdah - same root as Yadah but more specific - hand extended in adoration, approval or acceptance

Shabach - to shout, to address in a loud tone, to command, to triumph

Barak - to kneel down, to bless God as an act of adoration

Zamar - to pluck the strings of an instrument, to sing, to praise

Tehillah - the singing of Halal's, to sing or laud, singing

Exercise 3-2 (page 25)

1) Greek

2) Because it's in the New Testament, and because the Strong's number starts with a "G"

3) G3308

4) merimna

5) None, just "care"

6) Yes

7) G3309 - merimnao

8) (have) care, (be) careful, take thought

Exercise 3-3 (page 26)

A) You would look up all the references to "Spirit" and "Ghost" and compare the Greek words used.

B) He discovered they are the same and there is no difference between them, because the Greek word for "Spirit" is "pneuma" (G4151), the same word used for "Ghost."

Exercise 3-4 (page 26)

A) The Greek word for "sorceries" is *pharmakeia* (G5331), which is obviously a cognate of our English word "pharmacy." In the days of the New Testament, practitioners would use hallucinogens to enter an altered state so they could perform their sorcery. With drug abuse as prevalent as it is in our society today, the biblical prohibition against "sorcery" is still relevant when it is understood correctly.

Exercise 5-1 (page 34)

B) You should have found 18 unique verses in the New Testament

Exercise 5-2 (page 35)

A) 20 uses in 18 verses (used twice in 1 Cor 7:34 and 1 Pet 5:7)

Care = Mt 13:22; 1 Cor 12:25; 2 Cor 11:28; Php 2:20; 1 Pet 5:7

Careful = Lk 10:41; Php 4:6

Cares = Mk 4:19; Lk 8:14; Lk 21:34

Careth = 1 Cor 7:32, 33, 34, 34; 1 Pet 5:7

Take Thought = Mt 6:25; Mt 6:31, 34; Mt 10:19; Lk 12:22

Exercise 5-3 (page 38)

A) *dynamis* and *exousia*

B) G1411 and G1849

C) *dynamis* = miraculous power, *exousia* = ability, mastery, authority

D) *dynamis* = ability, abundance, meaning, might, mightily, mighty, mighty deed, etc.
   exousia = authority, jurisdiction, liberty, power, right, strength

E) Even though the word "power" is used for both, dynamis speaks of power while exousia speaks of authority

Exercise 6-1 (page 44)

1) Abel was a prophet (Mat 23:24,25 & Mk 11:50,51)

2) By faith Abel made his offering (Hebrews 11:4)

3) He's dead, yet he still speaks to us today (Hebrews 12:24)

Exercise 6-2 (page 44)

1) Enoch's genealogy is confirmed (Luke 3:37)

2) By faith Abel was translated into Heaven (Hebrews 11:5)

3) He was a prophet, and we have part of what he prophesied (Jude 14)

Exercise 7-1 (page 46)

Example Chronological Study Solution

The solution is to discover a way to harmonize all four of the Gospel accounts without compromising the integrity of the scriptures. It's helpful to remember that the Gospel of John was later written by the young man who was with Andrew that day (John 1:40), and both were disciples of the Baptist at first. John the author is describing what HE saw over those seven days.

A careful reading of John chapter 1 reveals that when Jesus appears on day 2, John the Baptist doesn't baptize Him at that point, he just recognizes Jesus as He approaches, and recalls when he saw the Spirit descend on Him earlier. "And I saw, and bare record that this is the Son of God." (vs.34). John has already baptized Jesus in water, and seeing Him approach reminded him of something that has already happened (vs.29).

So if John had already baptized Jesus, that means the events Matthew records (echoed in Mark and Luke) took place exactly as described. As Jesus' 40 days of temptation were coming to an end, the young future author, John, was watching his preacher hero, John the Baptist, arguing with the Pharisees. The "next day", when the 40 days of temptation had ended, young John was there to witness Jesus' return to the Jordan River where the Baptist was still ministering. The day after that, Jesus met John and Andrew who left John the Baptist to become Jesus' first disciples.

Exercise 7-2 (page 48)

(Note: Some of these are subjective answers. Your answers may vary.)

A) Goliath

B) Gath, a city of Philistia

C) It probably upset them.

D) It's hard to make sense of it. Why would David act that way? Why would he pretend to be crazy?

E) It helps the reader to better understand why David feared the people there.

Exercise 7-2 (page 48) - continued

F) This Psalm is beautiful, encouraging, and empathetic.

G) 1 Samuel 21 shows what is happening to David outwardly, while Psalm 56 shows what is happening to him inwardly.

H) Knowing the background helps to place Psalm 56 in its actual context.

I) Putting Psalm 56 in its chronological setting moves it from the abstract into the real world.

Exercise 8-1 (page 50)

A) The Apostle Paul

B) In prison

C) Rome, where Paul was imprisoned

D) The original audience was Paul's protégé, Pastor Timothy

E) Approximately 67 AD

F) Paul's arrest and travel to Rome

G) Christians were being persecuted for their faith and false teachers were arising in the church

H) Paul was executed by Nero

I) The succession of Paul's ministry after his death

J) Roman paganism

K) The Jewish War had begun in Israel, and since Christians were seen by Rome as a sect of Judaism, they were persecuted also

L) Paul wanted to encourage Timothy to remain passionate for Christ and to stand firm in the faith

M) This book ties into the end of Acts and closes out the ministry of one of the greatest leaders in the 1st century church

Exercise 10-1 (page 61)

Suggested chapter divisions for 1 John chapter 1:

vs 1-13 - The Pre-Existent Christ
vs 14-18 - The Incarnation
vs 19-28 - Ministry of John the Baptist
vs 29-34 - The Witness of John
vs 35-42 - Jesus calls His first disciples: John and Andrew
vs 43-51 - Jesus calls His next two disciples: Philip and Nathaniel

How Can I Be Saved?

Are you ready to accept the gift of eternal life that Jesus is offering you right now? If you sincerely desire to receive Jesus into your heart as your Lord and Savior, then here's a suggested prayer you can pray. You don't have to use these exact words. What's most important is that you're talking to God from your heart:

"Lord Jesus, I know that I'm a sinner and I don't deserve eternal life. But, I believe You died and rose from the grave to make me a new creation and to prepare me to dwell in your presence forever. Jesus, come into my life, take control of my life, forgive my sins and save me. I now place my trust in You alone for my salvation and I accept your free gift of eternal life."

Congratulations! You've just been adopted into the family of God. Since the theme of this book is largely focused on the unseen spirit realm, let me make you aware of what the angels are doing right now, according to Jesus:

Just so, I tell you, there is joy before the angels of God over one sinner who repents. – Luke 15:10

If you've prayed this prayer for the first time, please contact us at

praisereport@michaeldorseyonline.org

so we can celebrate with you!

About the Author

Saved at the age of 10 and Spirit-filled at age 16, Rev. Michael Dorsey has been a Christian for more than 30 years, and a teacher of the Word of God for over 20 of those years. He has ministered to new believers one-on-one, taught various Bible courses, and has spoken at ministers conferences.

Michael is the author of several books, including the multi-volume *How To Live* series. He has been called of God to provide quality outreach materials for true seekers, to build up and strengthen new believers, and to train up mature Christians for more effective service.

His passion is discipling new believers, teaching them the Word of God so they can be transformed from victims into victorious Christians, and equipping those believers to then begin discipling others to the glory of God.

Michael and his wife Katherine, along with their children Robbie and Kirsten, are active partners with Riverside Church in the Baltimore MD area, where they work in the ministry and assist their Pastor to bless God's people.

THANK YOU!

I hope you've enjoyed this, the companion journal to *How To Study Your Bible,* the first book in the *How To Live* series. Now you're ready to take your Bible study to the next level of glory in Christ Jesus!

As a personal thank you for reading and using this copy of the *Sword Drills: Bible Exercises for the Spiritual Warrior,* I'd like to invite you to go to:

http://biblestudy.michaeldorseyonline.com

There you will find additional free resources available for download that will assist you further in your new career as a Bible student. If you don't yet have your copy of my book, *How To Study Your Bible,* I encourage you to order it today. It will greatly bless you. Learn more at http://biblestudy.michaeldorseyonline.com. Once again, thank you so much for your support and your prayers!

Michael Dorsey

Sword Drills
Bible Exercises for the Spiritual Warrior

is a publication of

MALAKIM P R E S S

For other books in
the *How To Live* series,
along with information on
new and upcoming projects
designed to equip Christians
to live in peace, joy, hope
and victory, please visit:

www.malakimpress.com

www.ingramcontent.com/pod-product-compliance
Lightning Source LLC
Chambersburg PA
CBHW081521040426
42447CB00013B/3298